DICTIONARIES OF WORLD RELIGIONS

BUDDHISM

Peggy Morgan

B T Batsford Ltd   London

Typeset by Tek-Art Ltd, Kent
and printed in Great Britain by
R J Acford Ltd
Chichester, Sussex
for the publishers
B T Batsford Ltd
4 Fitzhardinge Street
London W1H 0AH

ISBN 0 7134 5203 X

Acknowledgments

The Author and Publishers would like to thank the
following for permission to reproduce copyright
illustrations: Amaravati, Great Gaddeston, pages
11 (top), 30, 39 (top) and 43; Barnaby's, pages 21
(Mario Frova), 39 (bottom) (M. Ronson), 46
(George Sturm), 50 (Peter Larsen), 60 (bottom)
(G. Cubitt) and 66 (Hubertus Kanus); British
Museum, pages 7 (top), 14, 53, 60 (top) and 64;
Buddhist Society, pages 11 (bottom), 16 and 25;
Camera Press, pages 12, 23 and 32; Ceylon Tourist
Board, page 26 (bottom); Mike and Alison
Edwards, page 59; Zena Flax, pages 5, 13, 22, 42,
49, 52 (bottom) and 61; Werther Forman Archive,
pages 19 and 57; S. Foster, page 7 (bottom); Freer
Gallery of Art, page 22; Japan Information Centre,
pages 8 and 67; Mandel Archive, pages 3 and 35
(top); Mansell Collection, pages 9, 15, 17, 29, 33,
44 and 52 (top); C. Morgan, pages 41 and 63;
NSUK, page 51; Rissho Kosei-kai, page 48;
Victoria and Albert Museum, pages 10, 37,
and 55. The pictures were researched by Patricia
Mandel.

Frontispeice
Lay and monastic *sangha* gather for evening
prayers and meditation in front of the *stupa* at
Amaravati in Hertfordshire (*Zena Flax*).

Cover Illustrations
The colour photograph shows a gathering of the
lay and monastic Buddhist community in Britain
(*Zena Flax*); the two Thai children are chanting
devotional texts in honour of the Buddha in the
traditional posture of respect (*Barnaby's*); the head
of the Buddha from fourth- to fifth-century
Gandhara captures the peace and gentleness of the
Buddhist path (*Victoria and Albert Museum*).

Introduction

No single book whether large or small could possibly do justice to a religion which has affected major world cultures and transformed countless individual lives over 2500 years of world history. The Buddha claimed to teach the truth about the way things are, an ancient path not original to him and not limited to any one place and time. It is based upon simple precepts such as non-harming and a commitment to root out greed, hatred and ignorance in life. It has also produced great philosophical sophistication. Over the first thousand years of its history it spread from India as far east as Japan. In this century it has taken root in the West in all its forms.

This dictionary seeks to help those who are beginning to study Buddhism to investigate with ease the main terms and names that they encounter. This should be supplemented and enriched by as much contact with practising Buddhists as is possible.

The Languages of Buddhism

Buddhists have always been happy to translate their scriptures and to teach in the languages of the countries to which Buddhism has spread in the 2500 years of its history. This is a continuing process and Buddhist technical terms in Pali, Sanskrit, Tibetan, Chinese and Japanese are now being translated and transplanted into the languages of the West, such as English, French and German.

Although Theravada Buddhists prefer the Pali form for technical terms, English has tended to adopt the Sanskrit; for example, "Nirvana" rather than "Nibbana" and "dharma" rather that "dhamma". I have, therefore, given the majority of untranslated words in their Sanskrit form with reference to the Pali equivalent where necessary. Some names and terms are distinctive to particular forms of Buddhism; for example the title "Dalai Lama" for Tibetans, the name "Kwan-yin" in Chinese and the term "Zen" in Japanese. These have been left in the language in which they are most commonly used. To help with pronunciation I have written "sh" for the associated sound in Sanskrit rather than s or S which occur elsewhere – for example, "Ashoka" and "Shakyamuni". Since the dictionary is intended as an introduction for the general reader I have avoided using diacritical marks in transliterating from one language to another.

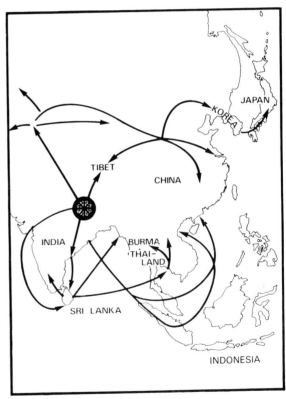

Map to show the spread of Buddhism in the first thousand years.

Abhidharma

The development of *abhidharma* began in the lifetime of Gautama Buddha. Over and above (*abhi*) the basic points of his teaching (*dharma*) there was always a further layer of explanation and analysis. Gautama Buddha and his followers clarified, elaborated and sorted out many points in his teaching into both psychological and philosophical schemes and lists of ideas. The description of a person in terms of five parts (*Skandha*) is one of the most famous examples of these analytical lists. Here is the analysis of right speech, one of the parts of the Noble Eightfold Path.

What is right speech?
1. Abstaining from false speech.
2. Abstaining from slanderous speech.
3. Abstaining from harsh speech.

4. Abstaining from frivolous speech.
What is abstaining?
. . . avoiding, desisting from, not commiting, not doing, being guiltless of, not overstepping the limit of, detroying the causeway to . . .
(From *Abhidhamma Vibhanga*, Section 2, Volume 3.39, Pali Text Society)

Abhidharma is still a living tradition amongst Buddhist scholars and teachers. Each Buddhist school or tradition has its own collection of *abhidarma* texts. The *Theravadin Abhidharma* was collected to make the third section of the *Pali Canon*, which is the collection of Buddhist scriptures in the Pali language. The third section is called the *Abhidhamma Pitaka* in Pali and the *Abhidharma Pitaka* in the Sanskrit spelling.
See also *Anatman, Eightfold Path, Tripitaka*.

Ahimsa

The best translation of *ahimsa* is "non-harming", although the phrase "non-violence" is sometimes used. When Buddhists take the first of the Five Precepts they commit themselves to not harming living things. In fact, the other precepts involve some kind of non-harming too. Harming anyone or anything intentionally is the same as hurting oneself. All life is interdependent.

All tremble at weapons, all fear death. Comparing others with oneself, one should not slay, nor cause to slay.
(Dhammapada v.129, tr. W. Rahula in *What the Buddha Taught*, Gordon Fraser, 1959)

Buddhists emphasize that the morality of an action is based on the intention behind it, and they know that people have to make decisions according to their circumstances. They try to live so that they do as little harm and as much good to the world as possible. This may mean being a pacifist or a vegetarian or not using industrial methods which will pollute the environment. Monks traditionally did not farm, because this involved taking life, but Buddhists are not dogmatic about how non-harming is carried out. The place where all outside actions begins is the heart and so it is important to cultivate *metta* ("loving kindness"). Just as harming is rooted in hatred, so non-harming is rooted in love.
See also *Metta, Precepts*.

Amitabha

This Sanskrit word means "having unlimited light"· It is the name of a cosmic *buddha*, who is also called Amitayus, having infinite or unlimited life. The Chinese translation of "Amitabha" is "A-mi-t'o" and the Japanese "Amita" or "Amida".

As Buddhism developed and changed, some schools did not concentrate on Gautama Buddha, but on other manifestations of the Buddha Nature. The cosmic manifestations had their own celestial *buddha* realms and could help people in various ways. There are five cosmic *buddhas*: Vairocana, Ratnasambhava, Amitabha, Amogasiddhi and Akshobhya.

Each cosmic *buddha* has his own story. Amitabha's story starts when, as a *bhikkhu* called Dharmakara, he heard Lokeshvaraja, the *buddha* alive then, teaching. He told Lokeshvaraja that he, too, wanted to be a *buddha*, and asked him for teaching, especially about the different *buddha* realms. He then concentrated and meditated for many aeons on the qualities of all the *buddha* lands, and when he became the *buddha* Amitabha his realm had the best qualities of all the others. It was a paradise in the West called Sukhavati ("The Land of Happiness-Having" or "The Pure Land"). This land is described in the *Sukhavati*

Sutras, which are the basic texts for the Pure Land schools of Buddhism. Those who meditate on Amitabha with good deeds and faith will be reborn in the pure land. Faith is expressed in the repetition of the name of Amitabha in the formula "Namu Amida Butsu", which is the *nembutsu*

("Buddha Name") in Japanese. Chanting this with faith gains rebirth in the pure land. Once the devotees are there the air is so full of *dharma* and Amitabha's teaching is so skilful that they are bound to attain Nirvana.

See also *Buddha Nature, Pure Land*.

Anagarika Dharmapala

David Hewavitarne (1865-1933) adopted this name at the age of 22 when he decided to devote his life to the revival of confidence in Buddhism in his native Sri Lanka and later to its renewal in India and its spread to the West. *Anagarika* is an adjective meaning "homeless". He chose it to show that he was devoting himself to Buddhism, without becoming a monk, but remaining active in the world. *Dharmapala* means "*dharma*-protector" (*dharma* is the term used for the Buddha's teaching).

Anagarika Dharmapala founded the Mahabodhi Society which is named after the Great Enlightenment Temple at Bodh Gaya in India. The society aimed to regain ownership of the site of the Buddha's enlightenment. The Mahabodhi Temple and many other of the great pilgrim sites associated with the life of Gautama Buddha were in a terrible state of disrepair. The society drew international support for their restoration and Buddhism in general.

See also *Bodh Gaya, Pilgrimage*.

This is a bust of Anagarika Dharmapala from the headquarters of the British Mahabodhi Society at The London Buddhist Vihara in Heathfield Gardens.

Anatman

In contrast to the dominant Indian belief in an eternal self or soul (*atman*) Gautama Buddha taught *anatman* (Pali: *anatta*), "not-self" or "no-soul". He was happy to use the term "person" or "self" in a conventional way, to refer to one living thing as distinct from another, but he denied that there is an eternal or immortal entity or part in people which will not change or decay and which will survive death. The destiny of living things was Nirvana, a state beyond any of the concepts we use of this life.

He asked people to look at the various parts that make up what they call "I" or the ego. He said that we can divide it into five parts, aggregates or "heaps". The Sanskrit term for these is *skandhas* (Pali: *khandhas*). The five groups are the body, feelings, perceptions, volitions or intentions of the mind, and consciousness. Not one of these groups can be identified with an eternal soul and the analysis does not leave room for a soul or self. A being is a combination of mental and physical parts

which work together in a chain of cause and effect without being permanent or unchanging. Some images help to show how the language of "self" works.

Gautama Buddha compared it with the sound of a lute:

A king, enticed by the sound of a lute, asks his servants to bring him the sound. They bring the lute, but the king exclaims "Away with the lute. I want the sound." The servant tries to explain: "This thing called a lute is made up of a great number of parts . . . it makes a sound because it is made up of a great number of parts; this is a box, strings etc." The king then takes the lute, breaks it up into smaller and smaller pieces, and throws it away . . .
(*Samyutta Nikaya* v. 196-8, quoted by S. Collins in *Selfless Persons*)

A different image is used when the monk

Nagasena questions King Milinda about the existence of his chariot by asking him whether it is the axle, wheels, chariot body, reins etc. The king realizes that the word "chariot" is used when all these other parts come together.

Nagasena also talks to Milinda about the way in which every part of the "person" has changed, both physically and mentally, between a baby, child, young and old man. What we call the person is the chain of life, the continuity of one becoming another.

People sometimes find it difficult to understand that the Buddha denied the existence of an eternal essence in human beings at the same time as teaching that there is rebirth and an ultimate state called Nirvana. Nagasena again provides two helpful images. There is a continuity between sweet milk, sour milk, butter and *ghee* (clarified butter), but they are not the same. There is also the idea of flames on lamps.

> While the flame of a lamp does not move over from one wick to another, yet the flame does not because of that fail to be produced, so too, while

nothing whatever moves over from the past life to this life, nevertheless aggregates . . . do not fail to be produced here, with aggregates . . . in the past life as their conditions, or in the future life with those here as their condition.
> (*Visuddhimagga XIX*, v.22).

The flame image is useful because it links with the most common language for Nirvana, and the root of the word itself, which is the blowing out of a flame, or the cooling of a fire. It is when the flames of desire have died down, and the suffering caused by grasping after self has gone, that Nirvana is reached. When there is no longer any sense of self there is no feeling of separation from others and no fear for the self or fear of dying. People then become selfless. To see things as they really are is to acknowledge what Buddhists call the Three Marks of Existence: the world as unsatisfactory (*dukkha*), impermanent (*anitya*) and not-self (*anatman*).

See also *Impermanence, Nirvana, Rebirth, Suffering*.

Arhant

An *arhant* is "one who is worthy", or "holy one", for whom the term "saint" is sometimes used. The word is Sanskrit, the Pali equivalent being *arhat*. In Theravada Buddhism it describes the highest spiritual level a person can reach, the state of enlightenment itself. After death an *arhant* will not be reborn but will attain final Nirvana. *Arhant* can be used as an additional title for a *buddha*. The

term *arhant* is also used for people who become enlightened through hearing the teachings of a *buddha* and are unconcerned about the enlightenment of others. In Mahayana Buddhism they are then contrasted with *bodhisattvas*.

See also *Bodhisattva, Buddha, Mahayana, Theravada* .

Art and Architecture

The characteristic architectural form in Buddhism is the *stupa*, which is based on the burial mounds covering the ashes of Gautama. *Stupas* have developed into a variety of styles in different Buddhist cultures and have become the pagodas of China and Japan. Miniature reliquary *stupas* in crystal or precious metal and jewels were buried inside the main *stupas* or placed in shrine rooms. The *stupa* was also used as a symbol of Gautama's death in carvings and paintings.

Most Buddhist buildings and works of art have been donated by kings, merchants and the families of members of the *sangha* to "make merit". A typical inscription reads "May the merit of this work bring salvation to the donor's parents and to all living creatures." The artists who made the work, who were often monks, usually remained

anonymous.

The earliest carvings are on the railings and gateways of the surviving *stupas*. Favourite topics are the Jataka tales and the life of Gautama. He is represented in symbols rather than in human form at this stage. A *bodhi* tree stood for his enlightenment, a wheel for the first sermon, a *stupa* for his death and an empty throne or footprints for his presence generally. The state of enlightenment, or Nirvana, which he had reached was not only difficult to express in words but also to portray in a human image. It was not until the first century C.E. in Mathura in the Ganges-Jumna valley and in Gandhara in north-west India that art forms were found to portray the Buddha with a human image.

A particular feature of Buddhist art is the rock-cut monasteries which were built in India at sites such as Ellora and Ajanta between second century B.C.E. and seventh century C.E. and along the silk trade route and into China at places such as Tun-huang and Lung-men. They provide storehouses of painting and sculpture and have produced other finds, such as the ninth-century copy of the *Diamond Sutra*, the oldest printed book in the world.

Massive stone figures all over the Buddhist world give the onlooker a sense of awe and an impression of the stillness and stability that is part of the Buddhist teaching about Nirvana. Particularly impressive is the 14.6-metre-long statue of the Buddha reclining at death at Polonnaruwa in Sri Lanka.

Devotees are shown in the same postures that are used today to venerate the memory of the Buddha. He is represented symbolically by a *bodhi* tree, three parasols, an empty throne and two footprints on which are carved wheels of the *dharma*.

The figure in front of the table for flower offerings is dwarfed by the massive 14m long and 8m high portrayal of the death of the Buddha. The sculpture conveys both great strength and calm in the face of death. It is at Polonnaruwa in Sri Lanka and dates from the twelfth century C.E.

In Tibet Buddhist art stayed close to that of Hindu India. The colourful figures of the *bodhisattvas* and *buddhas* are portrayed with many arms and the male and female forms together are important in the tantric tradition. Many of the important figures, *mandalas* (sacred diagrams) the Wheel of Life and the *lama* lineages are painted on wall hangings called *tankas*, which are a distinctive feature of Tibetan art.

In China and Japan the *stupa* form made its most radical development into the *pagoda*. Both China and Japan have a rich tradition of painting on silk, and scenes such as Amida's Pure Land have received a great deal of attention. Also notable are the exquisite porcelain figures of the *bodhisattva* Kwan-Yin, where the medium is so appropriate for suggesting her gentle feminine compassion. There are also many large wooden sculptures of Avalokiteshvara. Calligraphy was used in China and Japan both as an accompaniment to painting and on its own. Especially in the Zen schools, the skilful use of as few strokes as possible and the technical control that this involved became a vehicle for and expression of enlightenment, the empty circle being used as a symbol of Nirvana. Other forms of art, particularly associated with Zen, are *ikebana* (the art of flower arranging), the art of gardening and the making of pottery for the tea ceremony. Potentially every ordinary article and activity could be made and used so mindfully that it could become a high art form in its simple perfection. All of these sought to show the spiritual path of Buddhism through quite ordinary activities, everyday objects and natural things.

Nothing has been said so far of the art of the book in Buddhism. The first scriptures were written by hand on dried palm leaves, and the development of the Sinhalese Pali script is linked with the way the leaves are grained. In Tibet the oblong paper texts are stored between wooden boards which are carved with appropriate scenes and symbols. In China a common form for the scriptures was the scroll. It was in China that wooden type-blocks were first used to print the scriptures. The oldest printed book in the world is a copy of the *Diamond Sutra*, printed from wood blocks in 868 C.E. Manuscripts were not only copied with great care and aesthetic sensitivity but were also decorated and illustrated. It was mainly in the monasteries that the scriptures were copied, printed, stored and studied and it was the *Sangha* that in general preserved the traditions and made the cultural adaptations necessary for Buddhist art to thrive.

See also *Mudra, Stupa, Tankas, Wheel of Life*.

The simple harmony of raked sand, rocks, trees and wooden temple buildings provides a helpful environment for meditation in Zen Buddhism. The forms in the garden suggest both the patterns of the universe in which we live and the ripple effect of our minds as they act upon the world.

Ashoka

Ashoka inherited the Mauryan empire in India in about 270 B.C.E. At first he made war as was expected of a king in those days, until the violence and bloodshed of one campaign sickened him. He became interested in religious teaching, or *dharma*, and decided to try to rule the country with virtue rather than force.

The sources for our knowledge of Ashoka are firstly the edicts which he had inscribed on columns and rock faces. These were not deciphered until the last century. He used them to teach morality to the people. Special *dharma* officers were appointed to read them out and see that they were followed. Ashoka says in the famous twelfth rock edict that he

> honours members of all sects . . . by doing this one strengthens one's own sect and helps the others, while by doing otherwise one harms one's own sect and does a disservice to others . . . Concord is best, with each hearing and respecting the other's teachings.
> (Quoted by L. Stryk in *World of the Buddha*, Doubleday Anchor, 1968)

The second source of our knowledge of Ashoka is the Buddhist legends. To Buddhists he is the supreme example of a pious Buddhist layman, a Buddhist ruler and a person on the way to enlightenment. He was the first Buddhist ruler and was responsible for Buddhism becoming a world religion, dispatching missionaries both throughout India and abroad. He sent his son and daughter to Sri Lanka and presided over a Buddhist council at his capital, Pataliputra, in about 250 B.C.E. He is said to have built not only roads, but also thousands of *stupas* all over India as visual reminders of the Buddha's path.

See also *Dharma*, *Stupa*.

This is the top of one of the pillars set up by Ashoka on which he engraved *dharma* teachings for the people. The top is decorated with animals and *dharma* wheels.

Avalokiteshvara

This is the Sanskrit name for the *bodhisattva* who personifies the infinite compassion of the Buddha Nature. He is closely linked with Amitabha, who is usually drawn at the top of Avalokiteshvara's headdress. The name "Avalokiteshvara" probably means "the lord" (*ishvara*) who looks down (on the sufferings of beings in Samsara).

In Chinese and Japanese Buddhism the manifestation of compassion is in female form and is called Kwan-yin and Kannon. These names seem to mean "the one who hears the sounds" (probably the cries of a suffering world). In Tibetan this *bodhisattva* is called Chenresig.

Avalokiteshvara has a special connection with Tibetan Buddhism. He is the country's patron and protector and is believed to be reborn in many of its famous figures, including the Dalai Lamas. The great *mantra* of Tibet, "*Om Mani Padme Hum*", is said to have been the gift of the *bodhisattva*. Each syllable represents a realm of being which he purifies. Avalokiteshvara is often pictured in a thousand-arm form. The thousand helping hands each have an eye to see what is needed and each holds an object helpful to those in need.

See also *Amitabha, Bodhisattva, Compassion, Dalai Lama, Mantra, Tibetan Buddhism.*

The gentle compassion of Avalokiteshvara is captured in the white procelain figures made in China of her in the feminine form of Kwan-yin.

Bhikkhu

This is a Pali word (Sanskrit: *bhikshu*), which originally meant "almsman", and describes those Buddhists who followed the example of Gautama Buddha in renouncing the world and living on the gifts (alms) offered them by the laity. The term *bhikkhu* is usually translated into English as "monk". They can also be called "sons of the Buddha" and collectively the community of monks and nuns is known as the *sangha*.

Theravada monks wear saffron-coloured robes, Tibetans maroon and the Zen community black. They all observe a *vinaya* code of conduct. The Theravada code is contained in the *Vinaya Pitaka* of the *Pali Canon*. The following description applies mainly to the Theravada tradition.

There are two stages of ordination for monks and nuns. The first is as a novice, following the Ten Precepts, and then there is higher ordination which is only possible after the age of 20. The monk traditionally had eight basic possessions although variations, in robes for example, are allowed because of differing climatic conditions. Buddhism has always permitted a compassionate middle way avoiding rigid extremes, so there must be flexibility. Everything a monk eats, wears and uses is a present from lay Buddhist followers who think that the presence of *bhikkhus* as teachers and guardians of the Buddhist *dharma* make them worthy objects of generosity.

A characteristic sight in Theravada countries in the early morning is the line of saffron-robed *bhikkhus* walking in silence on the almsround with their bowls on their shoulders. They are not

Meditation is often said to be the "work" of a monk. Here is a Zen monk sitting in meditation in a shrine room.

These Theravada monks in Thailand depend on the generosity of lay Buddhists for their food.

allowed to ask for food. The laity must be ready to offer it, and to thank the monks for this opportunity of making merit. Monks eat only one main meal a day and this must be over before midday. This gives them the rest of the day for meditation, study, teaching and practical tasks. They have two main functions: to meditate for their own salvation, and to preserve and teach the *dharma* for the salvation of others. Even in the Theravada tradition, however, there are different lifestyles. The forest monks live in remote parts and spend most of their time in a strict but simple rhythm of life focussed on meditation. Village monks spend more time on activities at shrines and in pastoral involvement with the laity. There are also scholarly monks who write books and teach in universities.

See also *Dress, Meditation, Ordination, Precepts, Sangha, Three Jewels, Vinaya, Women.*

Birth

There are no specifically Buddhist ceremonies to be observed at the birth of a child. The parents may make merit and blessings on this kind of occasion by asking monks to come to their home and chant *paritta*, the texts which are thought to give blessing and protection. They may also give food and other gifts to the *sangha*.

Bodh Gaya

The place of Gautama Buddha's enlightenment near Gaya in the modern state of Bihar in India. There is a famous temple there called the Mahabodhi ("Great Enlightenment") Temple and a descendant of the original tree under which the enlightenment took place. There are also other Buddhist symbols and works of art. The site was

A monk meditates outside the enclosure of the *bodhi* tree at Bodh Gaya. The tree is a descendant of that under which the Buddha gained enlightenment. The picture shows some of the pieces of cloth which decorate the tree and the lotus patterns and wheel of the *dharma* on the fence. The circular blocks of stone in the foreground contain symbolic footprints.

restored in this century by the work of Anagarika Dharmapala. It is one of the four great places of pilgrimage for Buddhists and there are many *viharas* for pilgrims run by national Buddhist groups from places like Japan, Sri Lanka and Tibet. Bodh Gaya has been called a microcosm of the Buddhist world.

See also *Anagarika Dharmapala, Bodhi Tree, Gautama, Pilgrimage.*

Bodhi Tree

Literally this means "enlightenment" tree. It is the name given to the tree under which Gautama Buddha sat at Bodh Gaya on the night of his enlightenment. This type of tree is also called *ficus religiosa* ("sacred fig tree") *ashvattha* or *pipal*. It has heart-shaped, pointed leaves which are sometimes used in Buddhist art. There is a descendant of the original tree at Bodh Gaya, and cuttings and seedlings have been taken all over the Buddhist world for veneration. Any one of these can be called a *bodhi* tree.

See also *Bodh Gaya, Gautama, Pilgrimage.*

Cuttings from the original *bodhi* tree have been taken all over the Buddhist world. This one is being grown in Britain.

Bodhidharma

Bodhidharma is the legendary first patriarch or master of Zen Buddhism. His name means "enlightenment teaching". He travelled from India to teach in China, probably in the fifth century C.E., though sometimes a sixth-century date is given.

The stories that are told about him reflect the character and style of Zen Buddhism very vividly, whether or not they are historically accurate. The following story describes his meeting with Emperor Wu-Ti when Bodhidharma first arrived in Canton. Wu-Ti was already a committed Buddhist who had worked hard for the *dharma* in China.

The Emperor asked: "What merit have I gained by having innumerable temples built, sutras written down, and monks initiated, ever since I ascended to the throne?"

The Master answered: "No merit whatever."

The Emperor replied: "Why no merit whatever?"

The Master said: "All these are impure motives for merit; they bear the puny fruit of rebirth as a human being or a deva. They chase a figure like a shadow, but have no reality."

The Emperor said: "What then is true merit?"

He answered: "It is pure knowing, wonderful and perfect. Its essence is emptiness. One cannot gain such merit by worldly means."

Thereupon the Emperor asked: "What is the sacred truth's first principle?"

The Master replied: "Vast emptiness, nothing sacred."

The Emperor said: "Who is it that now stands before me?"

The Master replied: "I don't know."

(From the Chinese chronicle *Ching-te ch'uan-teng lu*, quoted by H. Dumoulin in *Zen Enlightenment*, Weatherhill, 1979)

The Emperor did not like Bodhidharma's abruptness and banished him to the north of China. The story has all the style of a Zen *koan* and was used in this way in later practice.

Bodhidharma always looks very fierce in the paintings of him. This later verse seems to be a good description.

13

His eyes are meteors
he flashes like lightning
a death-dealing knife
a life-giving blow.
(From *The Gateless Barrier* by Hui-k'ai [1183-1260], quoted by S. Beyer in *The Buddhist Experience*, Dickenson, 1974)

The tradition about Bodhidharma says that after a nine-year meditation in one position he lost the use of his legs. Special dolls called *daruma* dolls (*daruma* is another version of his name) are made of him in Japan. They are usually of painted wood with a rounded base and roll from side to side. This illustrates the nature of a Zen practitioner who has "seven falls and eight recoveries". Another verse says:

Such is life
Seven times down
Eight times up.

The dolls, like stories about Bodhidharma, are important teaching aids.
See also *China, Japan, Koan, Zen.*

This is a typical painting of Bodhidharma which shows his penetrating and humorous stare.

Bodhisattva

This title means "enlightenment being" (Pali: *bodhisatta*). It is used in two ways. Firstly, it refers to beings destined for enlightenment or buddhahood by virtue of many previous births and the merit they have made. In this sense Gautama is called a *bodhisattva* before his experience under the *bodhi* tree.

In Mahayana Buddhism it has a second, more technical, use. *Bodhisattvas* are those who take a vow not only to attain enlightenment for themselves but also to postpone their own entry into Nirvana to help others. There are many different ways of expressing the *bodhisattva* vow. Here is one of them.

May I not enter into Nirvana until I have brought all beings to supreme enlightenment.

This unselfish intention is thought to be the very highest ideal in Mahayana Buddhism, where it is often contrasted with the way of the *arhant*. Mahayana Buddhists in the Tibetan tradition take this vow like an extra precept to show that this state of mind is what they are working towards. One very famous *bodhisattva* is Avalokiteshvara, whose very nature is compassion.

Here is a description of a *bodhisattva's* state of mind.

May I be a protector for those without one
A guide for all travellers on the way;
May I be a bridge, a boat and a ship
For all who wish to cross the water.

. . . .

And until they pass away from pain
May I also be the source of life
For all the realms of varied beings
That reach into the ends of space.
(Shantideva, *A Guide to the Bodhisattva's Way of Life*, tr. S. Batchelor, Dharamsala, 1979)

There is a definite pattern or path for *bodhisattvas* to tread after they make their first vow. It is based on six perfections and ten stages. *Bodhisattvas* should be perfectly generous, virtuous, patient, energetic, meditative and wise.

See also *Arhant, Avalokiteshvara, Compassion, Generosity, Perfections, Precepts.*

Borobudur

The huge, terraced *stupa* at Borobudur on the island of Java in Indonesia has been called the greatest Buddhist monument outside India.

Buddhism was taken to Java in about the fifth century C.E. In about 800 the *stupa* was built on a natural hill site. It was a busy pilgrimage place until about 930 C.E., when the centre of political and social life in Java changed. It was then neglected and by the nincteenth century had been badly damaged by rainfall, earthquakes and subsidence and almost completely covered by undergrowth. In this century an international team of experts has worked to excavate the base, which was completely buried, and to restore and strengthen the upper terraces.

Buddhists usually circumambulate (walk round) *stupas* and other holy places to honour them and make a special connection with whatever they symbolize. Most *stupas* have a single path near the base, and pilgrims walk round it in a clockwise direction. At Borobudur the pilgrims can circumambulate the base and seven ascending terraces to the top of the *stupa*. The climb symbolizes their progress along the *bodhisattva* path from Samsara to Nirvana. The old Buddhist name for the site, Bhumi Sambara Budhara, means "the mountain of the accumulation of virtue in the stages of the *bodhisattva*".

The *stupa* is built on a large square base, the sides of which are 123 metres long. The 160 sculptures on the stonework of the base provide pilgrims with a reflection of the world of sense-desire and pleasure with its consequences. This is a world that is left behind when pilgrims climb to the higher levels. The next stages are along four square terraces on which are carved scenes from the life and teaching of Gautama Buddha, the stories of his previous lives (Jataka tales) and the lives of other *buddhas* and *bodhisattvas*. The next levels are three circular terraces. On these there are 72 identical *stupas* in stone latticework, 32 on the first level, 24 on the next and 16 at the top. These give a feeling of simple harmony. Within each *stupa* is an identical meditating *buddha*. They illustrate the Buddha-Nature within all things which is hidden except to those who bother to look within. The climax of the climb and of the Buddhist's spiritual journey is a solid stone *stupa* of great simplicity, which is a dramatic contrast to the hectic scenes on the lower terraces. This represents the formless realm of Nirvana.

See also *Bodhisattva, Buddha, Jataka Tales, Nirvana, Pilgrimage, Samsara, Stupa*.

On the upper terraces of Borobudur one of the latticework stupas has been removed during restoration work to reveal the Buddha in the teaching posture inside it.

Britain

The development of Buddhism in Britain follows a pattern similar to that in other European countries such as Germany. Interest was first kindled by individual scholars and writers, who did much to provide basic information and texts. In 1879 Sir Edwin Arnold presented the story of Gautama Buddha's life in his *Light of Asia*. T.W. Rhys Davids became interested in Buddhism and learnt Pali while he was working for the Ceylon Civil Service and, together with his wife, wrote many books on Buddhism. In 1881 he founded the Pali Text Society, which continues to publish both texts and commentaries from the Theravada tradition. He was the first president of the British Buddhist Society which was founded in 1907 and which marks the beginning of a Buddhist community in Britain.

The first European to enter the *sangha* was British-born Allen Bennett McGregor, who had been ordained as a Buddhist monk in Burma with the name of Ananda Metteya. In 1908 he returned to England with three Buddhist monks.

Between 1924 and 1926 the Buddhist Society was re-constituted as the organization which still bears that name. In 1926 it produced the first edition of the journal *Buddhism in England* and its activities were boosted in 1925 by a visit from the Sinhalese Anagarika Dharmapala who oversaw the establishment of the British Mahabodhi Society in 1926. A *vihara* was also established in Hampstead.

The main influence at this time was the Theravada tradition but later, when the works of D.T. Suzuki were obtainable and when he visited England in 1935, it widened to include Zen. Christmas Humphreys, who was founder-president of the 1924 Buddhist Society and a dominant force in the British Buddhist community till his death in 1983, described most English Buddhists as

> Frankly eclectic [selective], choosing and using those principles found to be most helpful in their search for enlightenment.
> (Quoted in *Buddhism in England*, Buddhist Society)

The present Buddhist Society continues to be non-sectarian and its current journal, *The Middle Way*, includes articles and news of all the traditions. The Buddhist Society also produces a *Buddhist Directory* which shows the spread of Buddhist groups and communities. They range from the rural areas of Dumfries and Hertfordshire to such cities as London and Birmingham. Since

The Buddhist Society holds an annual summer school, which is attended by representatives from most of the main Buddhist groups in Britain. Here lay Buddhists offer food to both Zen and Theravada monks and nuns.

the Chinese entered Tibet in the 1950s many *lamas* have left their native land and the Tibetan tradition is now well represented in Britain. There are also Vietnamese Buddhist refugees. Both Soto and Rinzai Zen schools have centres and there is a small number of Pure Land Buddhists in addition to the Theravada groups. Learned monks from Burma, Sri Lanka, Thailand, Japan and Tibet advise and teach the rapidly increasing British Buddhist population. One group, called the Western Buddhist Order, and their supporters, called the Friends of the Western Buddhist Order, are trying to work out a distinctively British form of Buddhism. It is estimated that there may be as many as 100,000 Buddhists in Britain today.

See also *Anagarika Dharmapala, Theravada, Tibetan Buddhism, Vihara, Zen.*

Buddha

This is a title meaning "enlightened" or "awakened" one. References to The Buddha usually mean Gautama, who is given this title after his enlightenment under the *bodhi* tree. He is thought to be the *buddha* to teach this world aeon. There were other *buddhas* before him and the next *buddha* will be called Maitreya. The line of *buddhas* is infinite and we do not know them all. In Mahayana Buddhism cosmic *buddhas*, such as Amitabha, are also important. These are all manifestations of the same Buddha Nature and are united in their essence, the *dharmakaya*. Taking refuge in the *buddha* is the first of the Three Jewels of Buddhism.

See also *Amitabha, Buddha Nature, Gautama, Maitreya, Taking Refuge, Three Jewels, Trikaya.*

A massive Buddha image in the posture of meditation at Nara in Japan gives a sense of stability and peace to those who see it.

Buddha Nature

Buddhists teach that the true nature and destiny of all sentient beings is the state of enlightenment, or Nirvana. This can also be called the Buddha Nature. It lies like a seed within every living being and can also be symbolized by the image of a full moon, partly or totally hidden behind clouds. The different Buddhist practices all try to help people to realize this full potential and appreciate that they share the Buddha Nature with all other beings.

See also *Nirvana, Trikaya, Zen.*

Calendar

If Buddhists are using a strictly Buddhist dating they count the years from the birth of Gautama Buddha in 566 or 563 B.C.E. They will then put the letters B.E. for *Buddha Era* after the date. It is not easy to make a calculation of the current date, since the years are not the same length as in the Western, Gregorian, calendar. Most Buddhist countries have strictly lunar months and begin the year at different times, and many new years were not initially chosen for Buddhist reasons, although they now include Buddhist elements. For example, in Burma New Year is in April and originates in the cycle of fertility. In Japan it has been changed to 1 January so that Japan is in line with the secular West. In Tibet New Year is the same as in China, some time in January or February. The first day of the year must be on the second waxing moon after the winter solstice, and the festival lasts for half the month. Like the Chinese, the Tibetans associate each year with an animal and an element. The Buddhist folktale which explains the animal link recounts that at his death the Buddha called all the animals to him to say goodbye but only 12 came. To reward these 12 he named a month after each and they rotate in 12-year cycles. The special days in any year are usually associated with the full moon and, secondarily, with the new moon.

See also *Festivals*.

Causation

Understanding how things come to be as they are is very important in Buddhism. The doctrine of *karma* teaches that every deed, word and thought bears some fruit. The present is the fruit of the past and the seed of the future. On the night of his enlightenment Gautama realized how certain states lead to others in an interdependent chain. He understood the connections between things and how forces like ignorance and desire condition our lives. The teaching about his discovery is called the "Chain of Causation" or "Dependent Origination" (*Paticca-samuppada* in Pali). It is a 12-linked chain of cause and effect which is illustrated on the outer edge of the Wheel of Life. It is possible to start explaining the chain at any point relevant to a person's experience, but the links are usually listed in the following order.

1. Ignorance (blind person)
2. Habitual tendencies (potter at wheel)
3. Consciousness (monkey jumping about)
4. Psycho-physicality (man in boat)
5. Six-sense spheres (six-windowed house)
6. Engagement of the senses (an embrace)
7. Feeling (arrow in eye)
8. Desire (being offered tea)
9. Grasping (picking fruit)
10. Becoming (making love)
11. Birth (pregnant woman)
12. Suffering, old age and death (body carried to funeral fire)

It is this causal chain which provides personal continuity. Each link is a necessary condition for the next. When Nirvana is reached no more *karma* is made and there are no more conditions which cause another becoming, another birth. This is why Nirvana can be called the "not-made", the "not-become", the "unconditioned".

See also *Wheel of Life*.

China

Buddhism was taken to China and other parts of the Far East along the silk trade route by merchants and by monks who travelled with the caravans. They brought the forms of Buddhism which had developed in the central Asian oasis city states at that time, as well as influence from India. Literary records show that Buddhism reached China in the first century C.E., although the earliest remains probably date from the third century.

One of the most important aspects of the transplantation of Buddhism to China was the translation of Buddhist scriptures from Sanskrit to Chinese. Many of them were translated more than once and extensive catalogues of works were made. The translation work is associated with many famous names, such as Dharmaraksha, "the *bodhisattva* from Tun-huang", who worked in the second century C.E., and Kumarajiva (344-413), who came from central Asia to work in the Chinese capital, Ch'ang-an. The desire to have as many scriptural texts as possible motivated monks to travel along the dangerous route backwards and forwards between India and China as pilgrims and scholars. We have two remarkable accounts in the records of Fa-hsien who left China in 399 and returned in 414 C.E. and Hsuan-tsang who went in the seventh century. Wood-block printing techniques were developed to reproduce texts. The oldest printed book in the world is an illustrated copy of the *Diamond Sutra* in Chinese which was found in the caves at Tun-Huang; it dates from 868 C.E.

The transplantation of a religion, however, means more than the translation of texts. Every part of the religion has to be culturally adapted. Links were made between the Buddhist idea of the transcendent and the *tao* of Chinese Taoism. Avalokiteshvara became linked with the goddess of mercy, Kwan-yin. Fierce heavenly beings, the

Four Guardian Deities, became the kings of the four quarters who guard the *dharma*. The Chinese emphasis on the practical and the ordinary is part of the Zen path, as is the idea of naturalness. Morality (*sila*) became filial submission and obedience, and Nirvana was equated with *wu-wei* ("non-action").

The position of Buddhism in China was often precarious with local persecutions and changes of power. In 446-454 C.E. there was an intense period of destruction of buildings, images and scriptures by royal decree. The edict was revoked by the next emperor who tried to compensate by building the 20 cave temples at Yun-kang. There followed centuries when Buddhism became strongly established in China.

The move from India to China also produced new schools of Buddhism which emphasized different texts and practices. Some like Hua-yen, which no longer exists, and T'ien-t'ai (Tendai in Japan), were rather intellectual and *sangha*-oriented. Others, such as the Pure Land and Zen

A 15m high image of the Buddha carved in the huge rock-cut temple at Yun-kang in China which dates from the fifth century C.E.

groups, gained a great deal of popular support from the sixth century onwards and survived the major persecutions.

In 845 C.E. Buddhism in China received a terrible blow when the emperor thought that the Buddhist institutions had become too powerful. He ordered a census of the *sangha* and its property, and then decreed the confiscation of its lands, the melting down of metal objects and the return of monks to lay life. This was not a local act of persecution like earlier ones but over all China. Buddhism never really recovered its position, although there were later achievements, such as the printing of the whole Chinese Buddhist Canon in the Sung Dynasty (960-1279) and a revival of Pure Land in the Ming Dynasty (1368-1644). China was also the major source of development of Buddhism in Japan. There was another modest

Buddhist revival in the nineteenth century; but, on the whole, it was neo-Confucianism that dominated Chinese intellectual life from the ninth to the twentieth centuries. Nevertheless, in 1930 it is reported that there were 738,000 monks and nuns and 267,000 Buddhist temples in China and that

> Buddhism was not a prominent force in national life, but insofar as Republican China was religious, it was more Buddhist than anything else.
> (R.H. Robinson and W.L. Johnson, *The Buddhist Religion*, Wadsworth, 1982)

Communism became the dominating force in 1949 and was committed to ending all religious belief and activity. Property was again confiscated and monks and nuns forced to work. Many Chinese Buddhists went to live in Taiwan and Hong Kong to join existing Chinese communities there, and also in Malaysia, Singapore, the Philippines and North America. Many Buddhist temples and works of art were preserved as national treasures and in 1953 the Chinese Buddhist Association was re-created to provide a state-controlled framework for Buddhist links with overseas countries and internal Buddhist affairs. The Cultural Revolution (1965-9) brought another wave of persecution for all religious groups in China. The situation has again changed and since 1976 policies have been more liberal, but there are still general pressures to conform to Communism and a lack of economic support for religion. There is also considerable emphasis on modernization in all areas of life. These do not provide the most encouraging conditions for a re-flowering of Chinese Buddhism as an organized religion.

See also *Japan, Pure Land, Zen.*

Compassion

In Theravada Buddhism compassion (*karuna*) is listed as one of the four highest states of mind (*brahma-viharas*). The other three are loving kindness (*metta*), sympathetic joy (*mudita*) and equanimity (*upekkha*). Compassionate persons are free from hatred and ill-will. Their thoughts of compassion reach out to the whole world. A single word cannot really translate the full meaning of *karuna*. It includes supreme love, pity, mercy and compassion. *Buddhas* have very deep *karuna* for all beings and the *bodhisattvas'* thoughts of enlightenment arise from their compassion for, and identification with, the sufferings of others, whom they vow to help.

The earth, with its forests, great mountains and oceans, has been destroyed a hundred times by water, fire and wind at the close of the aeons: but the great compassion of a Bodhisattva abides forever.
Aryasura, quoted by H. Dayal in *The Bodhisattva Doctrine* (1932)

In Mahayana Buddhism compassion is particularly linked with the *bodhisattva* Avalokiteshvara, who is the patron of Tibetan Buddhism and in China and Japan has a female form as Kwan-yin.

See also *Avalokiteshvara, Bodhisattva, Mahayana, Metta, Theravada.*

Dalai Lama

Lama is the Tibetan equivalent of the Sanskrit word *guru*, which means "religious teacher". *Dalai* means "ocean" or even "great ocean" in Mongolian and is a Mahayana Buddhist image for wisdom, which is as great and all-embracing as the ocean itself. Great Ocean Lama was the title given in the sixteenth century by a Mongol leader to the chief monk of the Gelukpa school. In succeeding centuries this school became dominant in Tibetan religion and politics, so their chief *lama* also had a special position. The title was applied retrospectively to Gedungrub (1391-1471), who became the first Dalai Lama. The line is believed to continue through a series of reincarnations which are traced with great care and according to certain conventions. At the time of the Great Fifth Dalai Lama (1617-82) the belief was established that the Dalai Lamas, as well as being reincarnations of their predecessors, were also manifestations of Avalokiteshvara, the great *bodhisattva* who is the special patron of Tibet. The Dalai Lama's palace at Lhasa was called the Potala after the mountain in southern India which was regarded as Avalokiteshvara's abode.

The present Dalai Lama (b.1935) is fourteenth in line of succession. He has been in exile in northern India since 1959. The Chinese invaded Tibet in 1950 and it became more and more difficult and dangerous for him and many other *lamas* and ordinary Tibetans to practise their religion and way of life freely, so many made the dangerous journey over the mountains into northern India. The Dalai Lama now has his headquarters in Dharamsala, north-west of Delhi. Although there is now more religious freedom in Tibet than in 1959 the Dalai Lama feels that he can serve his people and his religion better at the moment in exile.

See also *Avalokiteshvara, Tibet.*

Many pictures of the Dalai Lama show him enthroned and robed as the living manifestation of the *bodhisattva* Avalokiteshvara and leader of the Tibetan people. This picture captures his gentle compassion and care for all living things, a characteristic which strikes the people who meet him. The dog is a Lhasa Absu, the traditional breed that guarded the temple in Tibet.

Death

Buddhism teaches that "all is impermanent" and that "decay is inherent in all component things". Death is only the most extreme example of this principle.

> Dying. . . like coming to birth, is really a continuous process, going on steadily all the time. We die all the time, from moment to moment, and what is really there is a perpetual succession of extremely shortlived events. Death is not to be regarded as a unique catastrophe which happens when one existence comes to an end, but it takes place all the time within that existence.
> (E. Conze, *Thirty Years of Buddhist Studies*, Oxford, 1967)

This means that the ideal attitude of a Buddhist in the face of death is acceptance. It is believed that the dead are reborn according to their *karma* in one of the five or six realms of existence, or, if they are enlightened, they will go to the "deathless" realm of Nirvana. A person's state of mind immediately before death is very important in determining the state of rebirth. Family, friends and monks gather at the bedsides of dying people to recite scriptures and involve them in acts of devotion. In Tibet the Tibetan *Book of the Dead* is read to prepare the dying for the stages of transition involved in death.

Funerals are important in Buddhism. The remains are usually cremated after about three days. During that time and at the funeral monks are invited to chant scriptural passages and give some teaching. Relatives and friends are reminded of the impermanence of life. Some of the most important rites happen after cremation. There are ceremonies for transferring merit to the dead person. This is usually done by feeding the monks and giving them robes and also in symbolic water-pouring rites. Merit is also transferred on anniversaries after death. Other funeral customs vary from one Buddhist country to another.

See also *Karma, Merit, Nirvana, Rebirth, Wheel of Life.*

Dharma

The Pali spelling is "*dhamma*". It refers to the truth about the way things are, reality or the law of life. It is what the Buddha discovered at his enlightenment and what he subsequently taught people.

Summaries of the *dharma* can be found in the Four Noble Truths, the Noble Eightfold Path and the Chain of Causation. The *dharma* is one of the Three Jewels or Refuges of Buddhism.

The term "*dharma*", usually in the plural, also has the less technical meaning of an "object of mind" or "thing".

See also *Causation, Eightfold Path, Four Noble Truths, Taking Refuge, Three Jewels.*

Dharmapada

This is the title of one of the most famous and popular collections of Buddhist scriptures (Pali: *Dhammapada*). It is one of the books within the *Sutra Pitaka* (Pali: *Sutta Pitaka*) in the *Tripitaka* (Pali: *Tipitaka*). The sayings are in verse which makes them very memorable.

V. 5
Hatred is never appeased by hatred in this world,
it is appeased by love. This is the eternal law.

V. 183
Not to do any evil, to cultivate good, to purify one's mind,
this is the teaching of the Buddhas.

V. 223
Conquer anger by love, evil by good,
conquer the miser with liberality, and the liar with the truth.
(*Dhammapada*, tr. W. Rahula in *What the Buddha Taught*, Gordon Fraser, 1959)

V. 252
The fault of others is easily seen; our own is difficult to see. A man winnows others faults like chaff, but his own faults he hides even as a cheat hides an unlucky throw.
(*Dhammapada*, tr. S. Radhakrishnan, Oxford, 1950)

See also *Scriptures*, *Tripitaka*.

Dress

There is no distinctive form of dress for lay Buddhists although it is traditional in some Buddhist countries to wear white for religious observances such as meditation.

Buddhist monks and nuns do, however, dress distinctively. Their heads are shaved once a month to show that they have given up the usual worldly interest in good looks and vanity. The rule allows the monk three basic robes: an outer robe, an under-garment and a cloak. Nuns add to these a belt and a skirt. Shoes were originally considered a luxury, but Buddhists do not believe in extremes of asceticism, so shoes, jumpers and head coverings are allowed where necessary. The usual colour of the robes is saffron yellow in Theravada countries and a maroon red in Tibet. This depends on local dyes and availability. The clothes were originally supposed to be made of cloth given by the laity, which might be in complete lengths or small pieces. If no cloth was given to them the monks collected bits of rag wherever they could. The symbolism of pieced robes is still kept, even by Zen monks who wear traditional Japanese garments in black but usually have a small pieced square hanging round their necks.

It is interesting to talk to Buddhist monks about the colour of their robes. There are many different interpretations. Saffron is the traditional Indian colour for world-renouncers and some associate it with the practice of wrapping the dead in saffron cloth. The monk's renunciation of the world then makes him as "a dead man walking". This link with the dead might also come from the practice of gathering abandoned pieces of cloth wherever

These women members of the *sangha* in Britain are wearing the white robes of Anagarikas. They are carrying the brown robes they have made for their ordination to the stage of observing the Ten Precepts.

possible, and monks certainly meditated in charnel yards. This colour is also said to ward off insects in a tropical climate and saffron can be a reminder of autumn leaves – a sign of impermanence.

Here is an account by a Tibetan *lama* of the symbolic meaning of some of his traditional clothes.

'Before entering the monastic discipline, one must acquire a complete set of clothing, from the cap down to the boots, and also a number of other special articles. These are not very attractive; but each is rich in meaning,

The ceremonial dress of Tibetan Buddhist monks is more elaborate than their ordinary dark red robes. It can include red or yellow hats, depending on the sect, heavy brocade capes and crowns decorated with the five *buddhas*.

specifically with regard to casting off the suffering of the round of rebirth (*Samsāra*), and the attainment of the joy of liberation (*Nirvāna*).

Take, for instance, the monk's boots. They symbolize the three mental poisons and their eradication. These poisons are attachment, hatred and confusion. The shape of the boots bears a resemblance to a rooster, a snake and a pig. They have a curved-up tip symbolizing the snout of a pig; on both sides of each shoe are two bumps resembling the upper part of a rooster's wing; and the curve from the top to the tip of the boot is like the curve of a snake. Buddha spoke of these three animals as being symbolic of the three mental poisons. The pig stands for confusion, the rooster for attachment and the snake for hatred. He declared that all suffering in the world arises in dependence upon these mental distortions. The monk wears them on his feet, symbolizing his suppression of the poisons and is thus reminded always to avoid them.

The boots themselves, aside from their symbolic significance, are neither comfortable nor stylish. In fact, when first seeing them, one is likely to think they are the boots of a barbarian. The reason for their unattractiveness is to counteract attachment for them. Most harmful actions are due to attachment; so there is a great need to prevent its arisal.'
(Tr. B. Wallace in *The Life and Teaching of Geshe Rabten*, George Allen & Unwin, 1980)

There are various groups of people, with their distinctive clothing, who live within Theravada monasteries in the West. Anagarikas, both men and women, take the Eight Precepts and wear white robes. Men who have taken the Ten Precepts are novice monks and wear saffron robes like those who are fully ordained. Women who have taken the Ten Precepts wear brown robes. At the moment women cannot be fully ordained.

See also *Bhikkhu, Ordination, Precepts, Women.*

Eightfold Path

In Gautama Buddha's first sermon he laid down the basic framework of Buddhist teaching in the Four Noble Truths and the Noble Eightfold Path.

The last of the Four Noble Truths is that a path to the ending of suffering does exist. It elaborates three basic areas: *sila* ("ethical conduct"), *samadhi* ("mental discipline") and *panna* ("wisdom"). The path is not meant to be followed in strict sequence but all the areas developed at the same time. This can be seen in the case of wisdom. A right view and an understanding of the suffering and impermanence of the world will motivate people to set out on the path, but such understanding will only be complete at a very advanced stage. So wisdom is both at the beginning and the end and develops along the way. Each of the stages is "right" in the sense of appropriate to one's situation.

Wisdom
Right Understanding is the perception of the world as it really is, without delusions. This involves particularly understanding suffering, the law of cause and effect, and impermanence.
Right Thought involves the purification of the mind and heart and the growth of thoughts of unselfishness and compassion, which will then be the roots of action.

Ethical Conduct
Right Speech means the discipline of not lying, not gossiping or talking in any way that will encourage malice and hatred.
Right Action is usually expanded into the five precepts: avoid taking life, stealing, sexual misconduct, lying and taking intoxicants.
Right Livelihood is a way of life which avoids causing harm or injustice to other beings.

Mental Discipline
Right Effort is the mental discipline which prevents evil arising, tries to stop evil that has arisen, and encourages what is good.
Right Mindfulness involves total attention to the activities of the body, speech and mind.
Right Concentration is the training of the mind in the stages of meditation.

See also *Five Precepts, Four Noble Truths, Gautama, Meditation, Wisdom.*

Emptiness

The words we use to describe what we know about life are often inadequate. Sometimes we have to find a very abstract term to make a profound point. The word "emptiness" is used rather like "space". Space is within, between and around everything and yet we can only say more about it by saying that space is where nothing else exists.

In Buddhism the most basic use of the word "emptiness" (Pali: *sunnata*; Sanskrit: *sunyata*) is in relationship to the false idea that there is any permanent, eternal soul or self in beings.

> As empty one should look upon the world,
> . . . being ever mindful.
> When he has destroyed the theory of a self,
> Then will be overcome death.
> (*Sutta Nipata*, v. 1119)

Buddhists teach that it is important to see things as they really are and that everything in the world is devoid of independent existence and permanent essence. Everything depends on something else for its existence and changes all the time.

> As stars, a fault of vision, as a lamp,
> A mock show, dew drops, or a bubble,
> A dream, a lightening flash, or cloud.
> So should one view what is conditioned.
> (*The Diamond Sutra*, V. 32a, tr. E. Conze, Buddhist Wisdom Books)

To be really wise is to be empty of illusions and false views of things. This wisdom sees emptiness as the true nature of the world. The selfless persons who know the true nature of life are empty of greed, empty of hatred and empty of illusions. Their state of peaceful clarity is the state of enlightenment itself, and can also be called Nirvana.

See also *Anatman, Nirvana, Suchness.*

Enlightenment

Enlightenment is a state of perfect understanding, of being awake to the true nature of life, its purpose and its end. This is what Gautama attained under the *bodhi* tree and it is the ultimate goal of all

Buddhist practice. Gautama summarized and tried to communicate his understanding in the teaching on Causation, the Four Noble Truths, the Eightfold Path and the Perfections.

See also *Buddha, Causation, Dharma, Nirvana, Perfection.*

Festivals

Each Buddhist country has a slightly different cycle of festivals or their own national names and customs for the celebrations observed by their particular Buddhist tradition.

The normal activities at festivals are very much like those described in the section on worship. Householders visit the *vihara* to make offerings of flowers, light and incense before the buddha images and also present the monks with food and other gifts. The monks chant the scriptures appropriate for the theme of the festival, lead the meditation and give some teaching.

In Theravada Buddhism the most important festival is the one which celebrates the birth, enlightenment and death of Gautama Buddha. The name of the festival, Wesak (pronounced "Vesak") or Wesaka-Puja, is taken from the lunar month in which it occurs, which is April/May in Britain. The celebrations should be on the full moon but in Britain the Buddhist community chooses the nearest Saturday or Sunday so that everyone is free and can travel to a Buddhist centre to be together.

At the time of Gautama Buddha, the wandering monks were criticized by the farmers for walking through the flooded fields during the rainy season and accidentally damaging the young rice shoots. To avoid this, and also because it was difficult for the monks to move about and teach in the rains, the Buddha told them to stay in one place during these three months. This period is called the Rainy Season Retreat (Vassa). It falls in the British months of June/July to October/November. The beginning and end of the retreat are marked as festivals. The day before the retreat begins is called Asalha-Puja and commemorates Gautama Buddha's first sermon. At the end of the Vassa there is a special ceremony when the householders give the monks the main items they will need for the next year, for example cloth for robes. This ceremony is called Kathina.

Another interesting Theravada festival is the "Magha-puja", again named after a lunar month which in this case overlaps with the British January/February. It marks a gathering of 1250 *arhants* to hear the Buddha's recitation of the

Dana ("giving"), usually in the form of sharing food, is an important part of all Buddhist festivals. The most meritorious giving is that to the *sangha*, which is pictured here.

pratimoksha, the core of the rules for the monastic life.

In addition to these major religious festivals, each Theravada country has its own New Year celebrations in the spring with many pre-Buddhist elements. There are also distinctive occasions, such as the Tooth Relic Festival in August at Kandy in Sri Lanka, or Poson, which celebrates the bringing of Buddhism to the island in the third century B.C.E. The Maha Jat (Great Birth Festival) in Thailand focusses on the Jataka tale of the previous birth of the Buddha, which is acted out and sung. In Burma there are various local pagoda festivals and every initiation is marked with considerable festivity.

Mahayana Buddhist countries such as Japan and Tibet each have their own New Year. Royal Losar in Tibet is at the same time as the Chinese New Year in the British February or March. In Lhasa, the capital of Tibet, the demonic powers of the old year are conquered by masked dancers, and monks make huge butter sculptures of Buddhist figures and symbols which the cold climate preserves for the 15 days of the festival. At New Year Tibetans visit each other and give each other presents, including gifts of food and clothing to the monks.

The rest of the Tibetan religious year includes celebrating the birth, enlightenment and death of the Buddha on the fifteenth day of the fourth lunar month, and remembering his first sermon on the fourth day of the sixth month. Another special day marks the Buddha's visit to his mother when he was still a child to preach to her in the heaven where she had gone after her death. Mothers are very important in Tibetan culture, where the teaching about compassion involves the idea of loving all beings as if they were one's mother.

In Japan New Year coincides with that in the West. On New Year's Eve, the temple bells, which symbolize the passing of time and impermanence, ring 108 times, for the evils of the old year and the blessings of the new. The birth, enlightenment and death of Gautama Buddha, or Shakyamuni as he is usually called in Japan, are celebrated on separate days. The birth is marked in April at a flower festival, Hana Matsuri. Models of the Lumbini Gardens, where the Buddha was born, are set up in the courtyards of temples and the children bathe a little image of the standing baby Buddha with perfumed water from a ladle. The enlightenment is marked at Jodo-e in December and the death at Nehan-e in February. Higan, the "other shore" days at the spring and autumn equinox, focus on the state of Nirvana and are spent by many in the natural peace of temple gardens. At Obon in July mothers and other ancestors are remembered when people visit their families and home villages for outdoor games, fairs and the making of religious offerings.

See also *Calendar, Gautama, Initiation, Worship*.

BUDDHA DAY

Everyone is invited to participate in the Buddhist Society/Amaravati joint celebration **18th May, 1986, starting at 10.00 a.m.** at Amaravati, Great Gaddesden, Herts.

It is hoped that this will be a truly interdenominational Festival, with all the different traditions that reside in the U.K. joining in, and conducting their own festivals.

All are welcome!
Please bring Dana-food offerings for the Sanghas

PROVISIONAL PROGRAMME

9.30 am	Arrive at Amaravati
10.30 am	Open invitation to all lay visitors to take the **FIVE PRECEPTS**
10.30 am	Offering of food to the Sanghas
11.00 am	Shared meal
1.00 pm	Ceremonies by different traditions
2.00 pm	Ceremonies at the Stupa
3.30 pm	Talks by distinguished guests
5.00 pm	Tea

Free transport will leave the Busabong Restaurant 329-331 Fulham Rd., London SW10 at 7.45 am

For information contact Ray Percheron c/o The Buddhist Society.

A notice which appeared in *The Middle Way* in May 1986. The Theravada festival of Wesak is made into a "truly interdenominational" occasion.

Drummers outside the Temple of the Tooth in Kandy, Sri Lanka, prepare for the processions at the Tooth Relic Festival. In the background is one of the ceremonial elephants which will be decorated to take part in the procession.

Four Noble Truths

These were taught by Gautama Buddha in his first sermon. They summarize the core of his teaching and are basic to all Buddhist schools. They are noble in the sense of being spiritually profound. The way in which the Truths are given is often associated with the image of the Buddha as a doctor. He describes the condition of the patient, diagnoses the cause of the disease, says that a cure is possible and prescribes that cure.

The four Truths are:

1. All is suffering (*dukkha*). This suggests that the basic problem of the world is that we find it unsatisfactory. It is the first of the three marks of existence and claims to be a realistic analysis of the nature of life in *Samsara*.

2. The origin of *dukkha* is thirst (*tanha*), which is a vivid image for desire and greed. This grasping after sense pleasures, power, opinions and beliefs and the slavery to *Samsara* which it brings is so basic to Buddhist teaching that it recurs as one of the three root evils, *Three Fires*, in the centre of the Wheel of Life and in the Chain of Causation round its rim.

3. There can be cessation or extinction (*nirodha*) of *dukkha* and *tanha*. The image here is that the fire of desire and the suffering that it causes can die down and be extinguished. This quenching of the fire is Nirvana, the ultimate goal of Buddhists.

4. There is a path (*magga*) which leads to the *nirodha* of *dukkha* and *tanha*. This is the Noble Eightfold Path, which is then described.

See also *Eightfold Path, Nirvana, Suffering, Three Fires, Three Marks of Existence.*

Four Signs

The traditional stories of Gautama Buddha's life describe how he was brought up in the comfort and security of a beautiful palace and park. His father took care that he did not see anything that was ugly or in pain because there had been predictions at his birth that if he did he would leave home and become a wandering religious teacher.

When Gautama was a young married man, however, he became curious and restless to see what life was like outside the palace grounds. He persuaded his charioteer to drive him out of town. There he saw what are known as the Four Signs. They completely changed his life.

The first sign was an old man. Gautama asked whether everyone grew so old and frail, and was shaken when his charioteer answered "Yes".

The second sign was a man who was very ill. Gautama asked his charioteer whether he too might ever be sick. When the charioteer answered that nobody is free from the possibility of sickness Gautama began to think how fragile life was.

The third sign was a corpse being carried to be cremated. Gautama was again upset and discussed with his charioteer that it was the destiny of all living things to die.

The fourth sign was a man dressed in the saffron robes of a homeless holy man. The charioteer told Gautama that this man hoped to find the true meaning of life, and a happiness that was permanent.

After seeing these signs Gautama could not settle down again to his comfortable life. He felt that he had to leave home and find the cause of suffering and a cure for pain and sorrow.

See also *Dukkha, Four Noble Truths, Gautama.*

Gautama

The names and titles of the "historical *buddha*" often cause confusion. He is commonly referred to by the family name of Gautama (Pali: Gotama). His personal name, Siddhartha, is not found in the *Pali Canon*. The title Shakyamuni ("the sage of the Shakya tribe") distinguishes him from other *buddhas*. In the period before his enlightenment he is called a *bodhisattva* ("a being on the way to enlightenment") and another title, *tathagatha*, is interchangeable with *buddha*.

Buddhist tradition says that Gautama Buddha lived for 80 years. The popularly accepted dates among Western scholars have been about 566-486 B.C.E., but strong argument is now being made for dates at least 100 years later from about 448-368 B.C.E. The setting is north-east India in the small kingdoms of the Gangetic valley. The main events form a pattern and example for Buddhists and the accounts contain poetry and legend added to a core of historical fact. The *Pali Canon* does not contain a continuous life story; this was left to later writers. His birth is seen as the last in a long chain of lives

The Buddha is said to have been born from his mother's right side in the beautiful Lumbini gardens. The tradition may recall a birth by Caesarian section. His mother died shortly afterwards.

during which he was preparing for enlightenment. The stories of his progress in previous lives are told in the Jataka tales.

It is recounted that on the night of his conception his mother, Queen Maya, dreamed that a white elephant – a rarity, so a sign of an exceptional being – entered her womb. The birth itself is said to have been without pain in the beautiful Lumbini gardens. Gautama is said to have been born out of his mother's right side, to have walked seven steps immediately after his birth and to have been bathed in perfumed water by the Indian gods.

After his birth, court astrologers told his father, King Suddhodana, that he would be either a world ruler or a great religious teacher as a result of encountering suffering. His mother died soon after his birth and he was brought up by his aunt, Prajapati, who later became the first Buddhist nun. As he grew up his father tried to protect him from seeing suffering by restricting him to the palace grounds. Gautama married a beautiful princess called Yasodhara and they had a son called Rahula. Despite his happy and protected life Gautama became restless and persuaded his charioteer, Channa, to take him outside the palace grounds. There he saw what are called the Four Signs: an old man, a sick man, a corpse and a wandering holy man. The impact of these, with their message of change, suffering, death and the possibility of a search for the meaning of life, had a profound effect on him and after a period of inner conflict he left his wife and child in the care of his family and set off into a homeless existence.

He was 29 years of age. He left his fine clothes and horse with his charioteer, cut off his long black hair with his sword, and wandered off. This is called the Great Renunciation and is the model for the ceremonies of initiation and ordination in Buddhist communities.

Gautama found two religious teachers who taught him all they knew of yoga and meditation. He still did not feel, however, that he had found the answer to his quest. Next he became fiercely ascetical (self-denying) and ate so little that he could feel his backbone through his stomach. He found this did not help him either and led to his idea that the right way was a middle one between the extremes of self-indulgence and self-denial. He began to eat some food and the five other ascetics he had been with thought he had become "soft" and left him. Gautama was now 35 years old and had been searching for six years. He decided to stay in a pleasant spot under a sacred tree at Bodh Gaya and meditate until he had found the answer to his search. Throughout a whole night he meditated in the lotus posture and faced the obstacles to his enlightenment which are described as a temptation by Mara, the personification of evil, and his daughters. With a downward gesture of his hand he asked the earth mother to bear witness that he was worthy of enlightenment through the perfections he had attained in his previous births, and Mara fled. Gautama then attained enlightenment and became known as Buddha. The state of enlightenment is difficult to describe. It is a clarity, a knowledge of the way things are which

is expressed in the Chain of Causation. It also involves a realization that there is ultimately no separate soul or self, the leaving behind of desire and rebirth and the attainment of a state of great peace, which is called Nirvana.

The story says that he thought that what he had realized would be too difficult to teach others but that Brahma Sahampati, the high god of Hinduism, entreated him to help beings out of their sufferings. He agreed to teach and went to the deer park at Sarnath near Benares (Varanasi) where he met the five ascetics who had been his companions. They saw a new radiance and authority in his face and listened while he preached the Four Truths and the Eightfold Path to them. They became his first followers. He travelled in the middle Ganges region teaching people for 45 years until he died at the age of 80, reclining peacefully between two *sal* trees at Kusinagara. This is called the *parinirvana*, or "entry into final Nirvana". His body was cremated and his remains placed in *stupas*.

See also *Bodhisattva, Buddha, Causation, Eightfold Path, Festivals, Four Noble Truths, Four Signs, Initiation, Jataka Tales, Mara, Middle Way, Pilgrimage, Stupa, Tathagatha.*

Just before his enlightenment Gautama was tested by the hosts of Mara who symbolize desire and anger. He touches the earth to ask it to bear witness to his worthiness, attained through many births, to the state of enlightenment.

Generosity

Giving (*dana*), or generosity, is one of the basic Buddhist virtues. It is the first on the list of Perfections and the opposite of greed.

The most common acts of generosity include the giving of food and robes to monks and nuns and money for Buddhist activities. The technical term *dana* is usually used for these acts. It is said:

> Five blessings accrue to the giver of alms, the affection of the many, noble association, good reputation, self-confidence and heavenly rebirth.
> (*Anguttara Nikaya 5, Sutta 34*, translated by Nyanaponika)

The monks return the generosity of the laity with *dharmadana*, the gift of the teaching of the Buddha.

> The gift of the law surpasses all gifts.
> The flavour of the law surpasses all flavours.
> The delight in the law surpasses all delight.
> (Dhammapada, v. 354, tr. S. Radhakrishnan, Oxford, 1950)

Robes are given to monks at the ceremonies which end the rainy-season retreat. This is the festival of Kathina.

As with all Buddhist actions the important part of giving is the intention behind the act, and if it is ever done for public praise the motive is marred.

See also *Bodhisattva, Jataka Tales, Perfections, Three Fires.*

Gods

Buddhists use the term "gods" for those beings who have earned a longer, more pleasant and powerful life than that lived in the world of men and women. The realm of the gods is one of the five or six realms in which one can be born. These can be seen as psychological states of mind rather than places. Gods are not immortal and the word "god" does not refer to a creator or a final and ultimate reality in the cosmos. Gods can be helpful. Brahma Sahampati persuaded Gautama to teach people after he became enlightened and Four Guardian Deities are often represented in Buddhist art.

See also *Enlightenment, Rebirth, Wheel of Life.*

Hinayana

This term is used in two different ways, the first of which can cause offence. When the movement called Mahayana Buddhism was developing it claimed that the variety and inclusiveness of its ideas and practices provided a great or big (*maha*) vehicle or boat (*yana*) to take beings across the sea of Samsara to Nirvana. Mahayana Buddhists said their way was superior to the older schools of Buddhism, which they called the *hina* (lesser or inferior) *yana* (vehicle or boat). There is only one of the older schools of Buddhism left, the Theravada. Theravada Buddhists are justly proud of preserving ideas, practices and texts which they claim to be the closest to those taught by Gautama Buddha himself, and they are very offended by the term *hinayana*, which should therefore be avoided in this context.

The other usage is that found amongst Tibetan Buddhists. They say that all the forms of Buddhism, including their own, have within them different levels. The terms they use for the levels are *hinayana*, *mahayana* and *vajrayana*. The *hinayana* is a way of steady self-discipline and refinement with a careful balance between strict moral norms and renunciations of the world. At the *mahayana* level the variety of methods for attaining Nirvana increases and there is an emphasis on the compassionate way of the *bodhisattva* and the skilful means necessary to help others. These two levels can also be called the *shravakayana* (the *shravakas* – "listeners" or "disciples" – were the first monks who followed Gautama Buddha), and the *bodhisattvayana*. The last level, the *vajrayana*, is then seen as the highest and fastest way to enlightenment where the initiative is under the special care of a teacher of this path.

See also *Bodhisattva, Mahayana, Theravada, Tibet, Vajrayana.*

Ignorance

Avidya (Sanskrit) or *avijja* (Pali) can be translated as "ignorance", "illusion" or "delusion". Along with greed and hatred it is one of the three basic evils in Buddhism and is portrayed as a pig or hog in the centre of the Wheel of Life and by a blind man in the Chain of Causation, which runs round its rim. The importance of ignorance in the Buddhist tradition is shown by the number of different times it occurs in the teachings. In the *Pali Canon* ignorance is defined as not knowing the Four Truths. It can also be equated with "wrong view", the opposite of "right view" which, together with "right understanding" makes up wisdom. Ignorance is said to be the last fetter which binds beings to the cycle of rebirth. Ignorance and desire together are said to be the outstanding causes of *karma*.

See also *Four Noble Truths, Three Fires, Wheel of Life, Wisdom.*

Impermanence

The teaching that all is impermanent is the most basic of the Three Marks of Existence. The Sanskrit term is *anitya* and the Pali *anicca*. The other two marks, suffering and not-self, are largely dependent upon the experience of constant change that is a fact of life in Samsara.

> Impermanency of things is the rising, passing and changing of things, or the disappearance of things that have arisen. The meaning is that these things never persist in the same way, but that they are vanishing and dissolving from moment to moment.
> (*Visuddhi Magga* VII.3 by Buddhaghosa, tr. Nyanamoli, Shambhala, 1976)

Many things in life remind Buddhists of this teaching about impermanence. The tinkling sound of temple bells disappears quickly into the air. The beautiful flowers that are offered in shrine rooms open, wither and die. The only reality that is beyond all suffering and change is Nirvana.

See also *Anatman, Nirvana, Suffering.*

Initiation

In Buddhist countries like Burma and Thailand optional initiation into adulthood takes the form of lower ordination, the ceremony for entering the *sangha* as a novice monk or nun. This generally happens between the ages of eight and twelve but it is possible for an initiate to be as young as four or as old as twenty. Because it involves expensive family celebrations it is common for families to group together and arrange a joint initiation. The children stay in the monasteries for varying lengths of time. It can be as little as a night, it can be a week, the whole rainy season or a few years.

The ceremonies vary according to local custom. The following are some of the common features. It is thought that performing them brings great merit to the families, especially in the feast and presents given to the monks. There is usually some kind of village celebration on the evening before initiation with non-Buddhist activities which bring purification and good fortune, music and a feast. On the initiation day the children are dressed as princes and princesses. This is to identify them with Gautama, who was a prince before he renounced the world. In Burma a palace structure is built and the monks are ceremonially fed there before a procession goes to the monastery. In the procession the initiates are carried or ride on animals. They have parasols held over them to show their royal status. Presents for the monastery and the robes that the children will need are all carried in the procession. Any musicians and guests can join in.

At the monastery the lower ordination continues in the usual way. As well as taking the Three Refuges and Precepts, the candidate asks for ordination, has his head shaved and changes into saffron robes. There is a sermon from the senior monk and a recitation of sacred texts. There is usually also a water-pouring ceremony to transfer merit and as a symbol of cleansing and purification. The new monk is honoured by the laity and then stays in the monastery for a short time. Since the order of nuns does not exist in its traditional form in Theravada countries the girls usually return straight home.

The term "initiation" could also be used for the ceremony which admits an adult into a religion for the first time. A person becoming a Buddhist recites the Three Jewels. This is called "taking refuge".

See also *Bhikkhu, Ordination, Taking Refuge.*

Burmese boys re-enact the renunciation of Prince Siddhartha by dressing up as princes (*below*), processing to the monastery and putting on the robes of novice monks (*above*). They then stay in the monastery for anything from a few days to years.

Japan

Japan's first contacts with Buddhism were at the end of the sixth century C.E. They came at first from Korea and later directly from China. Prince Shotuku (574-622 C.E.) was the official founder of Japanese Buddhism. Various Chinese schools were transplanted to both Korea and Japan and·many great monastic and cultural centres were established which are still places of interest and pilgrimage for the Japanese.

The Kegon school (Chinese: Hua-Yen) flourished at Nara from the eighth century and influenced culture at many levels. When the capital was moved to Kyoto the synthesis of Tendai Buddhism was established nearby at Mt Hiei. In the ninth century Kukai established Shingon (Chinese: Chen-Yen) at Mt Koya. He was later called Kobo Daishi. Both these schools were in some decline by the twelfth century and Pure Land, which had been included as part of the Tendai system, became a separate school under Honen (1133-1212). Jodo-shin-shu (True Pure Land) was established by Shinran (1173-1262).

The Nichiren (1222-82) schools also emerged in this period of social and political upheaval. In the same century Dogen established Soto Zen in Japan, while Eisai did the same for Rinzai Zen which was revitalized later by Hakuin (1685-1768).

The Shinto nationalism of the Meiji restoration in 1868 was hostile to Buddhism, but the religion has withstood the attempt to undermine its position in Japanese society. Twentieth-century Japanese Buddhism is characterized by renewals in the form of lay movements such as Rissho Kosei-Kai and Soka Gakkai and the international interest in Zen.

See also *China, Pure Land, Rissho Kosei-kai, Soka Gakkai, Zen.*

Any typical Buddhist temple or *vihara* is a complex of buildings. This is the oldest surviving Buddhist temple near Nara in Japan. Notice the tall *pagoda*, a development from the *stupa*, at the back. The other buildings contain living quarters for monks, a shrine room and a hall for meditation.

Jataka Tales

These are stories about Gautama Buddha's previous births or lives. Buddhists believe that only enlightened beings remember their former lives. The point of the stories is to illustrate and encourage moral perfections such as generosity, renunciation and patience. Attaining these perfections is an essential part of the path to buddhahood. The subjects are taken from the animal and human realms and overlap Indian folklore generally. They have been used to educate countless Buddhists and provide excellent material for teaching Buddhist ideas to Western children.

See also *Perfections*.

Karma

This word literally means "deed" or "action" and is spelt *"kamma"* in Pali. The doctrine of *karma* refers to a moral law of cause and effect; good deeds bear good fruit, either in this life or in a future rebirth, and bad deeds bear bad fruit. This teaching asserts that however unfair life seems at any given moment nothing is ever wasted. The present is the fruit of the past and the seed of the future. It is the intention behind an action which determines its consequences. For example, if a person plans to kill someone but never succeeds in actually doing it they are karmically guilty of murder. If, on the other hand, they kill someone without ever intending to, they do not reap the bad *karma* of murder though there is a less bad *karma*, that of negligence.

See also *Rebirth*.

Koan

The Chinese phrase *kung-an* means "old case" or "publicly announced document". It is *koan* in Japanese. *Koans* were originally the sayings or dialogues of famous Zen masters or teachers. They provided the case histories ("old case") or examples ("public document") of their teaching methods. These were collected, passed on and frequently used to test the progress and understanding of students, particularly in Rinzai Zen. They are kinds of word puzzles or riddles to be solved intuitively and often answered in actions rather than words. They are used to startle people intellectually, to encourage spontaneity and confidence and to teach the trans-verbal and trans-rational thinking which is characteristic of Zen Buddhism. There are many collections of *koans* made by Zen masters. Here is an example:

Chao Chou asked Nan Ch'üan: What is the Way?

Nan Ch'üan said: Your ordinary mind is the Way.

Chao Chou said: Then can I advance upon it?

Nan Ch'üan said: If you try, you won't.

Chao Chou said: But if I don't try, how do I know it is the Way?

Nan Ch'üan said: You cannot know it is the Way, & you cannot not know it is the Way. Knowing is mistaken, & not knowing is stupid. When you really penetrate the spontaneous Way, it is like a great emptiness, a vast openness: how can it be yes or no?

(From *The Gateless Barrier*, quoted by S. Beyer in *The Buddhist Experience*, Wadsworth, 1984)

See also *Japan, Zen*.

Kwan-Yin

See *Avalokiteshvara*.

Lotus

The Lotus flower is one of the most important symbols in Buddhism. The roots of the lotus grow in muddy water, which symbolizes Samsara. The flower rises up out of the water and opens out towards the sun. This growth and blossoming is taken as a symbol of spiritual growth and enlightenment. Just as there are many different coloured lotuses, so there are many different kinds of people.

In countries where lotuses grow, lotus buds are thought to be a particularly appropriate flower offering to make in a Buddhist shrine. Images of the Buddha and other works of art are often placed on lotus pedestals. The most common Indian meditation position is called the lotus posture. One of the most famous Mahayana Buddhist texts is called the *Lotus of the True Law*, or the *Lotus Sutra*.

Just as the lotus, though it is born in the water, and grows up in the water, yet remains undefiled by the water, just so should the strenuous monk, earnest in effort, remain undefiled.
(*Questions of King Milinda* vii. 2, 3, 4, tr. I. B. Horner, Luzac, 1964)

All men know suffering, which is the mud wherein the lotus takes root. All men know the lotus blossom which gazes at the heavens. Few men indeed know how to nourish the root of true religion in themselves in the mud of ignorance that surrounds them, and fewer still know how to make the root flourish and grow in the dark water the long stem that is needed before a flower can bloom in the clear light of day.
(J. Kennett, Introduction to Book 1 of *Zen is Eternal Life*, Dharma Publications)

See also *Lotus Sutra, Nirvana, Samsara*.

This engraving of a lotus flower shows its long stem and the graceful opening of its petals towards the sun.

Lotus Sutra

The Sanskrit title of this Mahayana scripture is *Saddharma pundarika* which can be translated literally as "The True Law Lotus". The *sutra* emerged in about 200 C.E. and has been especially influential in China and Japan. It claims to have been spoken by Gautama Buddha, but like other Mahayana *sutras* it is authoritative as a revelation of the eternal and omniscient Buddha Nature, developed in the *trikaya* ("three-body doctrine"), rather than the word of the historical Buddha.

The subject of the *sutra* is that all the different *yanas* ("vehicles" or "paths") of Buddhism, are in fact one *yana*, the *ekayana*. Any differences are to be seen as skilful devices, ways of adapting teaching to different types of people and situations. The *sutra* contains many interesting stories which illustrate this idea. A father wishes to save his sons from a burning house and in order to get them out promises them all kind of toys. His plan works but when they do emerge he has quite different and much better things for them. Another story is about a magic city conjured up by a guide to refresh travellers and help them to continue their journey,

॥ सद्धर्मपुण्डरीकसूत्रम् ॥

The title of the *Lotus Sutra* in Sanskrit (top) and Chinese (side).

35

but which disappears after they have rested in it overnight.

The *Lotus Sutra* has been the basic text for many Mahayana schools, for example the eclectic T'ien-t'ai group in sixth-century China which became Tendai in Japan. The thirteenth-century Japanese reformer Nichiren and all the sects which came from his work, such as the modern Soka Gakkai, Rissho Kosei-Kai and Nipponzan Myohoji, chant the title of the *Lotus Sutra* as a means of gaining enlightenment. In Japanese the *mantra* is "*Nam Myoho Renge Kyo*" ("Homage to the *Lotus Sutra*").

See also *China, Japan, Lotus, Mantra, Scripture, Trikaya.*

Mahayana

In the centuries following the death of Gautama Buddha, Buddhism developed into various sects and schools. *Maha* ("great") *yana* ("vehicle" or "way") is the name given to a whole group of ideas and practices which are basic to some of these schools. Mahayana claims to offer more possibilities for enlightenment than those groups which they critically called *hinayana* ("little vehicle"). These opportunities are based on three important ideas which are said to be continuous with the teaching of Gautama Buddha.

Firstly, people do not have to rely on their own efforts like the *arhants*, or necessarily become monks or nuns, but are helped towards enlightenment by *bodhisattvas* and cosmic *buddhas*. The ideal is to become a *bodhisattva* and postpone your own Nirvana in order to help others.

Secondly, *bodhisattvas* and cosmic *buddhas* use their skilful means to teach beings at all levels. This opens up all kinds of possibilities for Buddhist practice, from *koans* and *mantras* to ordinary activities such as hewing wood and drawing water, to act as vehicles for enlightenment. In Vajrayana Buddhism the term *mahayana* or *bodhisattvayana* is used for this second main level of practice.

The third development is the doctrine of emptiness, the belief that to the eye of wisdom, all distinctions between Nirvana and Samsara are ultimately empty.

Mahayana Buddhism is sometimes called "northern Buddhism" as these ideas underpin particularly schools such as the Pure Land and Zen in China and Japan and the different traditions in Tibet and Nepal. Each uses its own collections of scriptures as well as material from the *Pali Canon*. The main Mahayana texts emerged between 100 B.C.E. and 200 C.E. and include the *Prajnaparamita, Lotus, Vimalakirti* and *Sukhavati sutras*. They are used in Sanskrit, Tibetan, Chinese or Japanese and are believed to be buddha-word in one of two ways. Either they were spoken by Gautama Buddha and hidden until people could understand them, or they originate in the one Buddha Nature which emanates in all enlightened minds.

See also *Bodhisattva, Emptiness, Hinayana, Lotus Sutra, Prajnaparamita, Pure Land, Tibet, Vajrayana, Zen.*

Maitreya

Maitreya is represented as a bodhisattva who is waiting to be reborn in the world as the next Buddha after Gautama. The Chinese form of his name is Mi-lo. He is often identified with the tenth-century Chinese monk Pu-tai, who was a jolly, fat figure and symbolized the happiness and plenty it was hoped the age of Maitreya would bring. This identification has produced the "laughing Buddha" or Mi-lo-fo (*fo* meaning laughing).

See also *Gautama.*

Mandala

This Sanskrit word originally meant "circle", but is now a technical term for a sacred diagram. *Mandalas* are used in Tantric Buddhism, now mainly to be found in Tibetan practice. They may be painted on *tankas* ("scrolls"), made from coloured sand, constructed as a three-dimensional model, or just visualized; but always on the basis of the descriptive texts which control the conventions. They provide a kind of map of the spiritual and psychological world of the devotee, who moves in meditation through the doorways or directions represented on the edge of the diagram,

through different levels of understanding towards the centre. These levels are represented by various symbols within the *mandala* and lie within lotus forms, triangles, squares and circles. The purpose is identification with the powers and spiritual qualities of the central reality, emptiness, which is usually symbolized by a *buddha* or other personification.

See also *Gods, Tankas, Tibet.*

This sixteenth-century Tibetan example shows the square, circular and lotus patterns that are an important part of *mandala* symbolism. Gateways are visible on the sides of the inner square and various personifications in different parts of the diagram help the initiated to move to different levels of understanding.

Mantra

Mantra is a Sanskrit word meaning "instrument of mind" or "tool for thinking". It is a sacred utterance. *Mantras* can be a single syllable, a phrase, or a short text which is recited and used for protection, blessing or as an aid to meditation.

Mantras are used a great deal in Tantric Buddhism, which has sometimes been called the "Mantrayana" ("The *Mantra* vehicle"). Tantric Buddhism is now mainly known in its Tibetan form. The great Tibetan *mantra* is "*Om Mani*

Padme Hum", which is an invocation of the power and presence of Avalokiteshvara, the *bodhisattva* of infinite compassion. It is impossible to translate a *mantra* because every syllable is packed with meaning, but "*Om Mani Padme Hum*" is sometimes said to mean "Hail to the Jewel in the Lotus, Welcome".

Another famous *mantra* is that used in the Pure Land schools. In its Japanese form this is "*Namu Amida Butsu*", which is an invocation of the name of Amida Buddha. The Nichiren schools of Japanese Buddhism use the *mantra* "*Nam Myoho Renge Kyo*", which indicates respect for the law of cause and effect or devotion to the *Lotus Sutra*.

The *Heart Sutra*, which is already a highly condensed form of the Prajnaparamita teachings is further condensed into a *mantra* in its final phrases in Sanskrit: "*Gate, gate, paragate, parasamgate, bodhi svaha*". Perfect wisdom, and the enlightenment which it brings, are invoked as "Gone, gone, gone beyond, gone altogether beyond, O what an awakening, all hail."

See also *Avalokiteshvara, Japan, Prajnaparamita, Pure Land, Soka Gakkai*.

Mara

The personification of evil in Buddhism. Evil is whatever works against enlightenment. Mara is often identified with desire, anger and death and seen as a tempter. He is said to have sent his beautiful daughters to tempt Gautama Buddha on the night of his enlightenment, but the Buddha defeated them.

As the wind throws down a tree of little strength so indeed does Mara overthrow him who lives looking for pleasures, uncontrolled in his senses, immoderate in eating, indolent and of low vitality.
(*Dharmapada*, v. 7, translated by S. Radhakrishnan, Oxford, 1950)

See also *Gautama*.

Marriage

Getting married is embarking on the life of a householder. Householders are respected figures in all Buddhist societies and the *sangha* is materially dependent on them. They have their own code of ethics and follow the Five Precepts. However, in Theravada Buddhism it is thought that the life of a householder is not likely to lead to enlightenment. Marriage involves worldly goals and distractions, and a householder's religious life is to make merit for a better rebirth. This perspective has meant that there is no specifically Buddhist marriage ceremony in Theravada Buddhist countries.

The marriage ceremony is entirely secular. In itself it contains no Buddhist elements. On the morning of the wedding day, however, monks are invited to the home of the bride, where they are offered a special feast. Usually, but not always, they are asked to recite *paritta* (texts which bring protection and blessings) to protect the prospective bride and groom from danger. The monks return to their monasteries before the marriage ceremony begins: they do not even witness the ceremony, let alone take part in it.
(M. Spiro, *Buddhism and Society*, University of California Press, 1982)

In Mahayana Buddhism the attitude to marriage is rather different. The *Vimalakirti Sutra* and other teachings show that a householder can be enlightened. In Tibet some *lamas* are married and so are some temple priests in Japan. There is still, however, no specifically Buddhist marriage ceremony.

It is interesting that in the West, in societies which associate marriage with religion, attempts are being made to draw up Buddhist forms of marriage. At the time of writing, the Tibetan community at Samye Ling in Dumfries is licensed so that the legal and religious rites can be combined in one ceremony. Basically, the couple renew the *bodhisattva* vow together and receive blessings. Here is one of the prayers.

May there ever be goodness, reknown, great riches and all life's necessities in their finest of forms: great joy, bliss and happiness, strength, good influence and the very best material life which is long enduring, free of sickness and wherein all one's wishes are fulfilled.
(*Samye Ling: a Form of Marriage*, 1984)

See also *Mahayana, Precepts, Theravada*.

Meditation

The aim of Buddhist meditation is seeing the truth about the way things are and being at rest within it. All Buddhist schools have slightly different but related methods and all emphasize that a teacher is important.

A good image for the state of our minds is that they are like pools of water, all stirred up and muddy with feelings and thought. The point of meditation is first of all to let the mud settle and then when we can see the bottom, to look down and note what is there. The first stage for doing this is called *samatha*, ("calmness" or "peaceful abiding"). The body is relaxed in a stable position, which is usually cross-legged on the floor but for people who cannot manage that it can be on a chair. There are various ways of helping the mind to settle. One is by simple chanting and letting go of everything else. Another is the practice of watching and controlling the breath and constantly bringing back attention as it wanders to that calm point. When all the mud of activity has gradually settled in this peaceful concentration there is the second stage, that of *vipassana* ("insight", "clarity", or "penetrating vision"). Here one sees the emotions and thoughts that arise, the nature of

A forest monk meditates outside his hut.

The ideal of meditation is mindfulness at all times, whatever one is doing. Here a forest monk can exercise walking mindfulness as he carries his almsbowl over his shoulder.

the distractions and the general state of one's mind. One notes them and lets them go without creating more distractions by taking up thoughts and battling with them and stirring up the mud again.

Basic to both *samatha* and *vipassana* is the practice of mindfulness. This is a total awareness or alertness to the present moment, with no distractions. It can be brought to bear on any activity, but one of the most basic is walking mindfulness. There is a whole *sutta* in the *Pali Canon* on this practice.

Another important meditational practice is that based on *metta*. This builds on calm and insight to send thoughts of loving kindness outwards.

Whatever the methods followed, for Buddhists meditation is opening the door to an inner and outer pilgrimage.

See also *Metta, Mindfulness.*

Merit

Merit is the spiritual gain from certain attitudes and actions. It is a wholesome force which causes both happier lives and better rebirths. The attitudes and actions that are usually listed as merit-making are:

1 Giving, or generosity in general, but especially the giving of robes, food, a place to stay and medicines to the *sangha.*
2 Having faith in the Three Jewels, which are the *buddha, dharma* and *sangha.*
3 Leading a moral life, including service to others.
4 Practising meditation.
5 Listening to and helping to teach the *dharma.*

It is possible for a Buddhist to give away or transfer any merit that is made to others, for instance to friends and relatives.

At the end of many *pujas* and meditation sessions all the merit that has been made during the session is given away for the benefit of all conscious beings. The higher ideal is always to work for the good of others rather than one's own. The *buddhas* and *bodhisattvas* are the supreme examples of this selflessness.

The childish work for their own benefit
The buddhas work for the benefit of others
Just look at the difference between them.
From *A Guide to the Bodhisattva's Way of Life*, by Shantideva, tr. S. Batchelor, Dharamsala, 1981)

See also *Bodhisattva, Buddha, Dharma, Generosity, Meditation, Puja, Rebirth, Sangha.*

Metta

Loving kindness, goodwill and friendliness are all used to translate the Pali term *metta* (*maitri* in Sanskrit). *Metta* is the first of the *brahma-viharas* ("four highest states of mind"), the other three being compassion, sympathetic joy and equanimity. Together they form a basis for relationships to other beings and the world in general. In the *Pali Canon* there is a whole *sutta* (Sanskrit: *sutra*) on loving kindness. Here is part of it.

May all beings be happy and secure; may their minds be contented . . . .

Let not one deceive another nor despise any person whatever in any place. In anger or illwill let not one wish any harm to another.

Just as a mother would protect her only child even at the risk of her own life, even so let one cultivate a boundless heart towards all beings.

Let one's thoughts of boundless love pervade the whole world – above, below and across – without any obstruction, without any hatred, without any enmity.
(From *Metta Sutta*, tr. W. Rahula in *What the Buddha Taught*, Gordon Fraser, 1959)

The ideas in this *sutta* provide a basis for a type of meditation called "*metta* practice". In this, individuals or groups become mindful of what loving kindness is and concentrate on establishing it in their own hearts. From there they send it out to all corners of the world.

See also *Compassion, Maitreya, Pali Canon, Sutra, Three Fires.*

Middle Way

Before his enlightenment Gautama Buddha lived as a prince in great luxury. He then gave it up to become a strict ascetic. He found neither way very helpful for overcoming suffering and finding out the truth about the way things are.

> Self-indulgence is low, vulgar, ignoble and harmful, and self-mortification is painful, ignoble and henceforth both are profitless.
> (*Vinaya* 1.10ff. S.V.420ff)

It was only when he had tried a gentler way of meditation that he was enlightened. After his enlightenment he taught others a Middle Path or Middle Way between the extremes of self-indulgence and self-mortification. For example, a Buddhist monk is allowed adequate, but not luxurious, clothing, food and shelter. The Eightfold Path is an example of this Middle Way in practice.

In Mahayana Buddhism the Middle Way is expressed in a whole system of philosophy developed by Nagarjuna. *The Middle Way* is also the title of the quarterly journal of the British Buddhist Society.

See also *Eightfold Path, Gautama.*

Mindfulness

The *Pali Canon* contains a whole *sutta* on "mindfulness", called the *Satipatthana Sutta*. Mindfulness is a total alertness or awareness of the activity of the body, of feelings, of the mind and of the objects of thought. It is basic to the Buddhist's growth in understanding the truth about the way things are. It is linked with all kinds of meditation and with all daily life practices.

The basic teaching focusses on mindfulness of breathing, but it can be said:

> there is no mental process concerned with knowing and understanding that is without mindfulness . . . . Keep to mindfulness and clear comprehension in all activities, as in sitting, standing, walking, looking around and talking. He who has established mindfulness as a guard at the door of his mind, cannot be overpowered by the passions, as a well-guarded city cannot be conquered by the enemy.
> (Nyanaponika Thera, *The Heart of Buddhist Meditation*, Rider, 1962)

See also *Meditation.*

Monk

See *Bhikkhu.*

Mudra

Mudras are symbolic hand gestures which can be seen on the images of the *buddhas* and *bodhisattvas* in Buddhist works of art. Some gestures can be linked with events in the life of Gautama Buddha. In Tibetan Buddhism the *mudras* are used in some of the rituals. All Buddhists use the "hands together" gesture of reverence in one way or another. The main *mudras* are:

(1) *Bhumisparsha* ("earth-touching"). The figure in seated meditation has the right hand at the right knee pointing down to the ground. Linked with Gautama's appeal to the earth to bear witness that he is worthy of enlightenment during his battle with Mara.

(2) *Dhyana* ("meditation"). Hands together on the lap of figure in seated meditation, right on top of left. Often portrays Gautama Buddha at moment of enlightenment.

(3) *Dharmachakra* ("turning the Wheel of the Law"). The hands are held so that the thumbs and first fingers make circles. This illustrates Gautama

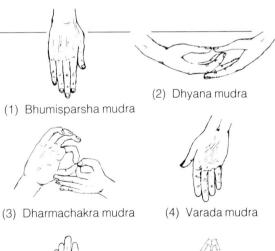

(1) Bhumisparsha mudra

(2) Dhyana mudra

(3) Dharmachakra mudra

(4) Varada mudra

(5) Abhaya mudra

(6) Anjali mudra

41

Buddha's first sermon in the deer park near Sarnath.

(4) *Varada* ("granting favour"). The hand is turned palm outwards and pointing down in a gesture of giving.

(5) *Abhaya* ("safety"). The right hand is raised, palm forwards, in a gesture of blessing and reassuring those present.

(6) *Anjali* ("hands together"). This is a gesture of respect or reverence which accompanies a bow, kneeling or prostration in front of a Buddha image or a revered teacher.

See also *Art, Gautama, Rupa.*

Nirvana

The root of this word derives from the image of a fire or flame and means "blown out", "extinction" or "cessation". To be in Samsara is like being trapped in a burning house, without even realizing it. The message of Buddhism is first of all like a fire alarm, to alert you to the fact that "all is burning" with the three fires of greed, hatred and delusion. When these fires die down and are extinguished the suffering of Samsara is at an end and there is Nirvana.

Trying to describe the state of Nirvana is as difficult as it is for a fish to describe the nature of dry land. The Chinese Buddhist Mou-tzu said:

If I could explain the essential meaning of Nirvana, it would be like speaking about the five colours to the blind or playing the five tones to the deaf.

Here are some other attempts to explain the idea from the *Pali Canon*.

As a flame blown out by the wind
Goes to rest and cannot be defined
So the wise man freed from individuality
Goes to rest and cannot be defined.
Gone beyond all images –
Gone beyond the power of words.
(*Sutta Nipata*, 1074-6)

There is a sphere which is neither earth nor water, nor fire, nor air, which is not the sphere of the infinity of nothingness, the sphere of neither perception nor non-perception, which is neither this world nor the other world, neither sun nor moon. I deny that it is coming or going, death or birth. It is only the end of suffering. (*Udana*, 80)

See also *Emptiness, Enlightenment, Samsara.*

Nun

See *Bhikkhu, Women* and *Sangha.*

Ordination

This is the ceremony for becoming a Buddhist monk or nun. At the time of Gautama Buddha there was a single act of "going forth" and taking on the full ascetic life under the *vinaya* rules. As Buddhism became a more institutionalized part of society, ordination was divided into two stages. "Lower ordination" can be taken between the ages of eight and 20. At the ceremony candidates take the Three Refuges and shave their heads, and after taking the Ten Precepts live within the monastic community as novice monks or nuns. The second stage can follow straight on for an adult over 20. This is called "higher ordination". The ceremony for this is conducted by at least ten *bhikkhus* and in the case of women by ten *bhikkhus* and ten *bhikkhunis*. The candidates must have two patrons who will be their companion and instructor in the monastic life. Candidates are asked whether they

Senior monks gather at the specially prepared *sima* or ordination area at Chithurst, Sussex, for an ordination ceremony. A Buddha image and a wheel of the *dharma* can be seen in the picture.

The basic symbol of ordination is "robing". Here an Anagarika is being given the saffron robes of a novice and full monk.

are free from disease, free of other commitments, have no outstanding debts, have their parents' permission and are at least 20 years of age. They must also have a set of robes and an almsbowl. The assembly is then asked three times whether there are any objections and if there is silence the candidate is considered ordained. The date and time of ordination is noted since that determines seniority in the order.

See also *Bhikkhu, Initiation, Ten Precepts, Vinaya*.

Pagoda

See *Stupa*.

Pali Canon

See *Tripitaka*.

Pali

The name of an ancient Indian language which is related to Sanskrit. The basic Buddhist scriptures were taken to Sri Lanka in Pali. Buddhist tradition says that this was in the reign of Ashoka in the third century B.C.E. and that they were written down in the same language in the first century B.C.E. This collection of scriptures is the one used by Theravada Buddhists and is called the *Pali Canon*.

Theravada Buddhists believe that Pali is the language spoken by Gautama Buddha, but this is disputed. Pali has no script of its own and so manuscripts in Pali may be written in, for example, Sinhalese, Burmese or Thai script.

See also *Ashoka, Sanskrit, Theravada, Tripitaka.*

Perfections

Paramita is usually translated by the English word "perfection", but it includes more than just moral qualities. It contains the idea of what has gone "beyond" conventional values towards enlightenment itself. Theravada Buddhism lists ten qualities or perfections leading to buddhahood: generosity, virtue, renunciation, wisdom, energy, patience, truthfulness, resolution, loving kindness and equanimity. They are all illustrated in the Jataka stories, showing how the Buddha lived out these perfections in previous lives.

In Mahayana Buddhism the list of perfections overlaps the above, but they are put in a different order and are only six in number: generosity, virtue, patience, energy, meditation and wisdom. They are particularly important in the development of the *bodhisattvas.*

See also *Bodhisattva, Generosity, Jataka Tales, Metta.*

Pilgrimage

At the end of his life Gautama Buddha recommended that his followers should visit four places: where he was born, where he became enlightened, where he first preached and where he was to die.

The place of his birth is Kapilavastu, which is in modern Nepal. The place of his enlightenment is Bodh Gaya, near Gaya in Bihar. The place of the first sermon (turning the wheel of the *dharma*) is in Sarnath, now a suburb of Benares (Varanasi) in Uttar Pradesh. The site of the Buddha's death is now disputed. The texts name the place as Kusinagara, or Kusinara, and it is often identified with modern Kasia in Uttar Pradesh, or it may be in northern Bihar.

These pilgrim sites all fell into disrepair or were taken over by other religious groups when Buddhism disappeared from northern India after the thirteenth century C.E. They have been and are being restored in this century, to a large extent due to the work of Anagarika Dharmapala. The most important of the sites is Bodh Gaya, which has been called both the centre and a microcosm of the Buddhist world. The main features of the site are a temple with a 59-metre tower in which there is an image of the Buddha at the moment of enlightenment. This is called the Mahabodhi ("Great Enlightenment") Temple. Nearby there is a descendant of the *bodhi* tree under which the Buddha was enlightened. Buddhists feel that a place like this has a great deal of spiritual power which is intensified by the constant flow of pilgrims. The national Buddhist communities such as the Japanese, Sri Lankan and Tibetan provide guest houses for pilgrims, and meeting other Buddhists from different parts of the world is

In traditional Buddhist cultures pilgrims were usually clearly recognized and respected. This Tibetan carries a staff to help him to walk and has prayer beads round his neck.

44

an important part of the pilgrimage. Pilgrims offer flowers, incense and light in the Mahabodhi Temple; sit in silent meditation near the *bodhi* tree; scatter flowers over the symbolic Buddha footprints set in stone discs on the ground; circumambulate the *bodhi* tree clockwise, a sign of respect for an important person at the time of the Buddha; and hang coloured prayer flags in the branches of the tree, both to honour it and leave their prayers behind when they leave.

It is not possible for all Buddhists to travel to India and pilgrimages are made to any site that has symbols of the Buddha's life or teaching. Even visiting a teacher can be seen as a kind of pilgrimage for a Buddhist. There are relics and *stupas* all over the Buddhist world. One of the most famous is the tooth relic in Kandy, Sri Lanka, round which there is a magnificent annual festival to which pilgrims might go. The Shwe Dagon Pagoda in Rangoon, Burma is continually covered in gold leaf by devoted laypeople. The great *stupa* at Borobudur in Java is terraced to provide a pilgrim path from its base to the top. The *bodhi* tree at Anuradhapura in Sri Lanka, taken there in the time of Ashoka, is another famous spot. Britain, too, now has its own share of *stupas* and pagodas and cuttings from *bodhi* trees.

The reasons why Buddhists go on pilgrimage are very varied. In Sinhalese a pilgrimage is called a "veneration journey"; the Chinese word for pilgrimage means "journeying to a mountain and offering incense". The Tibetan word for pilgrimage means "to circumambulate". To make the effort of a journey and undertake certain religious practices at a site is a way of making merit and also of bearing witness to what is really important in life. Seeing places where events actually happened can bring religious teachings vividly to life for a believer as well as satisfy historical curiosity. It is also thought that holy sites are a source of spiritual power which is bound to bring blessing on the devotee. It is enriching to meet Buddhists from other parts of the world and share experiences and fellowship. These are what can be grouped together as the reasons for the outer pilgrimage, the pilgrimage to a place. It must be borne in mind, however that the inner journey, the journey into the heart, is also important and that following the Eightfold Path is itself a pilgrimage.

See also *Anagarika Dharmapala, Bodhi Tree, Borobudur, Festival, Gautama, Merit, Stupa.*

Prajnaparamita Sutras

"Perfection of Wisdom" or "Wisdom Which Goes Beyond (Samsara)" is the name given to a whole group of Mahayana *sutras* which emerged from the first century C.E. onwards. They teach the distinctive ideas of the Mahayana, such as the *bodhisattva* path and the doctrine of emptiness. The earliest is the *Ashtasahasrika*, the perfection of wisdom in "8000 lines", which may be the oldest of all the Mahayana *sutras*. Here is its description of the *bodhisattva* path.

Doers of what is hard are the Bodhisattvas, the great beings who have set out to win supreme enlightenment. They do not wish to attain their own private Nirvana. On the contrary, they have surveyed the highly painful world of being, and yet, desirous to win supreme enlightenment, they do not tremble at birth-and-death. They have set out for the benefit of the world, for the ease of the world, out of pity for the world. They have resolved: 'We will become a shelter for the world, a refuge for the world, the world's place of rest, the final relief of the world, islands of the world, lights of the world, leaders of the world, the world's means of salvation.'

(*Ashtasahasrika* XV.293, quoted by E. Conze in *Buddhism: its Essence and Development*, Harper Torchbooks, 1975)

There are also texts in 25,000 and 100,000 lines. One of the most famous of the *prajnaparamita sutras* is the *Vajracchedika* ("*The Diamond-Cutter*"), which is in 300 lines. The diamond or thunderbolt (*vajra* in Sanskrit) is indestructible, like wisdom itself, and can cut through all convention and worldly logic. The *sutra* outlines the *bodhisattva* path and also teaches the boundless spaciousness of ultimate reality, which is empty of all separate being, and highlights the limitations of conventional experience and understanding.

As stars, a fault of vision, as a lamp,
A mock show, dew drops, or a bubble,
A dream, a lightning flash, or cloud,
So should one view what is conditioned.

The oldest printed book in the world is a copy of the *Vajracchedika* in Chinese, dating from 868 C.E. It was found in the Tun Huang caves early this century and is now in the British Museum.

The shortest *prajnaparamita* text is the *Hridaya*

("Heart Sutra"), which gives the core or heart of the teachings. The *sutra* is learned in Chinese or Sanskrit by many Buddhists and recited in worship and meditation. At the beginning of the text wisdom is greeted as a beautiful woman. "Homage to the Perfection of Wisdom, the Lovely, the Holy." At the end the teaching is further condensed into a *mantra:* "Gate gate paragate parasamgate bodhi svaha." *Mantras* are almost impossible to translate, but E. Conze in *Buddhist Wisdom Books* (George Allen & Unwin, 1958), gives the meaning in these words: "Gone, gone, gone beyond, gone altogether beyond, O what an awakening, all-hail."

See also *Bodhisattva, Emptiness, Mahayana, Mantra, Scriptures, Wisdom.*

Pratimoksha

See *Vinaya.*

Prayer Beads

Hindus, Buddhists and Sikhs all use the term *mala* for their circles of 108 prayer beads. ($108 = 2^2 \times 3^3$ was considered a round number with special astrological significance in India.) Buddhist prayer beads can be made of wood, of seeds from a sacred tree or even of plastic. If it is more convenient they can be half or quarter size (54 or 27 beads). They can be used to count the number of prayers or prostrations being made or as a deeper aid to meditation, either in private or by a group of people. The beads help to calm and concentrate the mind. With each bead the name of a *buddha* or *bodhisattva* is recited or remembered, or a *mantra* is said. There are often three larger beads within the circle which symbolize the *buddha, dharma* and *sangha.* The beads may be decorated with coloured tassels or Buddhist symbols.

See also *Mantra, Three Jewels.*

Prayer Wheels

Prayer wheels are a characteristic of Tibetan Buddhist practice. They are cylinders of wood, bone or metal and have written on them or inside them the *mantra "Om Mani Padme Hum".* Their association with this *mantra* also gives them the name *"mani* wheels". They can be small enough to be held on a handle in the hand and turned with a circular movement of the wrist. Larger ones are placed in shoulder-height rows along pathways to monasteries or shrines. These are turned with the hand as devotees pass them. They can also be in a shrine of their own and turned by water or wind power. In the west they are sometimes placed on electric turntables and driven that way.

The principle behind the turning of the *mantra* on the prayer wheels is the same as reciting it. It is being sent out to make merit, and to bless and transform the world.

See also *Avalokiteshvara, Mantra, Merit, Tibet.*

This Tibetan Buddhist is saying the *mantra "Om Mani Padme Hum"* with a prayer wheel in his right hand and prayer beads in his left.

Precepts

This is the technical term for the promises, vows or moral commitments that Buddhists make. They are usually taken in groups.

The Five Precepts are the basis for lay Buddhists:

1. I undertake the rule of training to refrain from harming any living things.
2. I undertake the rule of training to refrain from taking what is not given.
3. I undertake the rule of training to refrain from a misuse of the senses, i.e. unchastity.
4. I undertake the rule of training to refrain from wrong speech.
5. I undertake the rule of training to refrain from taking drugs or drinks which tend to cloud the mind.

The Eight Precepts are often undertaken by lay Buddhists on meditation retreats, at some festivals or *uposatha* days, and are basic for the group called Anagarikas in the English *sangha*. They include the first five precepts, with Precept 3 becoming "from all sexual activity", and three additions:

6. I undertake the rule of training to refrain from taking food at an unseasonable time, i.e. after the midday meal (lunch).
7. I undertake the rule of training to refrain from dancing, singing, music, and unseemly shows; from the use of garlands, perfumes, and unguents; and from things that tend to beautify and adorn (the person).
8. I undertake the rule of training to refrain from (using) high and luxurious seats (and beds).

The Ten Precepts form the basis of life for a novice monk, although there is only one new precept added to the eight above. Occasionally laypersons living in a monastic context will undertake these for a time, as with the eight.

7. I undertake the rule of training to refrain from dancing, music, singing and unseemly shows.
8. I undertake the rule of training to refrain from the use of garlands, perfumes, unguents, and from things that tend to beautify and adorn (the person).
9. I undertake the rule of training to refrain from using high and luxurious seats (and beds).
10. I undertake the rule of training to refrain from accepting gold and silver.

Most Buddhist ceremonies and meetings begin with a recitation of the Three Refuges and the Five Precepts.

See also *Ahimsa, Bhikkhu, Intention, Ordination.*

Puja

See *Worship*.

Pure Land

This is the most common translation of the Sanskrit term *Sukhavati*. A more precise meaning is "the land of happiness-having" or "well-being". *Sukha* is the opposite of *dukkha*, ("suffering").

It is said that all *buddhas* have realms, lands or spheres of influence. These can be talked about in different ways. In one way, since the *buddhas* are boundless, their realms exist wherever they have any influence. In another way the *buddha* realm is an inner, psychological, reality, which can also be described as a particular place. The Pure Land of Amitabha Buddha exists as a reality in the hearts of Amitabha's followers, but can also be described as a paradise in the West. It is not the final goal of life – this is enlightenment, or Nirvana – but a place from which Nirvana can be reached more easily because Amitabha is there with his skilful means to help you. It is described as being full of lotus flowers and jewel trees. Amitabha, haloed by the setting sun, welcomes his devotees there at death.

Pure Land developed as a separate school of Buddhism in China in the fifth century C.E. Buddhism was taken to Japan in the sixth and seventh centuries C.E. and later two schools of Pure Land Buddhism developed there. One of the schools is called Jodo-shu (Pure Land Sect). It was founded by Honen (1132-1212). The other school is called Jodo-shin-shu (the True Pure Land Sect) and was founded by Shinran (1173-1262). Members of these schools believe that Amitabha's compassion and enlightened mind shine out on all beings as a gift which activates and lights up the Buddha Nature within each of them. If they respond with faith in Amitabha's power and with good deeds (in the case of Jodo-shu) or even with just faith (Jodo-shin-shu), they will gain rebirth with Amitabha in the Pure Land. They are confident that once they are there Amitabha will help them to Nirvana. Their faith is expressed by the repetition of the name of Amitabha Buddha in the Japanese *mantra* "*Namu Amida Butsu*". This is the *nembutsu* (Buddha Name).

See also *Amitabha, China, Japan, Mantra, Suffering.*

Rebirth

All living things are part of a constantly changing cycle of existence. At the end of one life, if the *karmic* forces have not died out, they set in motion another life. This is like the energy sent from one billiard ball to another, or like one flame igniting another. Good *karma* leads to a better birth, bad *karma* to a worse. In Buddhism no substance or soul passes from one birth to the next. The chain of lives is linked together by the *karmic* forces. When the *karmic* forces have died out, the chain of becoming (Samsara) ceases and there is Nirvana.

Some enter the womb (are reborn on earth); evil doers go to a hell; the good go to a heaven; those free from worldly desires attain Nirvana. (*Dhammapada*, v. 126, tr. Radhakrishan)

See also *Anatman, Karma, Nirvana, Samsara.*

Rissho Kosei-kai

This is a new religious movement for lay Buddhists begun in Japan in 1938. Its co-founder and present leader, President Niwano, is interested in all forms of Buddhism and international problems. He has been awarded the Templeton Peace Prize.

The Japanese title "Rissho Kosei-kai" is packed with meaning, but a brief translation is "Society for Establishing Righteousness and Creating Fellowship".

Rissho Kosei-kai bases its teachings on the fundamentals of Buddhism expressed in the Four Noble Truths and the Eightfold Path but interprets these in the light of the *Lotus Sutra's* teaching on the essential oneness (*ekayana*) of the Buddhist ways and the *bodhisattva* path. Its object of worship is Shakyamuni (Gautama) Buddha, a large image of whom stands in the magnificent Sacred Hall of their headquarters in Tokyo. The application of the truths and path to everyday life is put into practice in daily counselling (*hoza*) sessions in small groups of up to 12 people, which is one of the characteristic activities of Rissho Kosei-kai. The practical involvement and social concerns of the movement can also be seen in its organization of schools, old people's homes, hospitals and youth schemes. The general approach of Rissho Kosei-kai is the application of Buddhism for the happiness, welfare and spiritual enlightenment of all beings. It is still mainly a Japanese movement, with some centres in other parts of the world.

See also *Four Noble Truths, Gautama, Lotus Sutra, Japan.*

Counselling groups help members of Rissho Kosei-kai to apply the Eightfold Path to their everyday lives.

Rites of Passage

See *Birth, Initiation, Marriage, Death*.

Samsara

The cycle of repeated birth, death and rebirth which is the state of all beings until they attain enlightenment. It is characterized by suffering, impermanence and not-self.

See also *Impermanence, Rebirth, Suffering, Three Marks of Existence*.

Sangha

Sangha means "assembly" and is the word used for the Buddhist community. The idea that its unity transcends time and place is expressed in the phrase *catuddisa sangha*, "noble community of the four directions". It is also possible to talk about the *arya sangha*, the "noble" or "ideal" *sangha*. This is one of the Three Jewels in Buddhism and is made up of those on the path to enlightenment.

Originally all Buddhists could be included in the term *sangha* in four groups: *upasaka* (layman), *upasika* (laywoman), *bhikkhu* (monk) and *bhikkhuni* (nun). These can also be called the sons and daughters of the Buddha. The *sangha* depends on the laity for gifts of food, clothing and shelter. In return its members preserve meditational practices and textual study and teach the *dharma*.

See also *Bhikkhu, Dharma, Ordination, Taking Refuge, Three Jewels*.

Here a whole community of Buddhist monks and nuns, laymen and laywomen are assembled. The laity are making offerings to the monks and nuns.

Sanskrit

The classical language of India in which the Hindu sacred scriptures are written. Many modern Indian languages are derived from it. The Buddha would have spoken a related regional dialect which is now lost to us. The Theravada canon of Buddhist scriptures was written down in Pali, another related regional dialect, but the Mahayana schools use *sutras* which were written in Sanskrit before they were translated into Chinese, Tibetan and Japanese.

See also *Mahayana, Pali, Pali Canon, Scriptures*.

Scriptures

The different Buddhist schools use different collections of scriptures. The most basic is the *Tripitaka* or *Pali Canon* that is used by the Theravada school. Theravada Buddhists are confident that this contains the words of Gautama Buddha. They believe the material was carefully collected soon after the Buddha's death and passed down accurately as oral tradition by trained monks until it was written down in the Pali language in Sri Lanka in the first century B.C.E. It is still studied and recited in its original language wherever possible although Buddhists are quite happy with translations when people do not know Pali.

Theravada Buddhists also respect and use works outside this canon. For instance in Sri Lanka in the fifth century Buddhaghosa wrote a famous summary of doctrine and practice called the *Visuddhimagga* ("Path of Purity"). There is also an important second-century C.E. dialogue between the monk Nagasena and the Greek King Menander ("Milinda" in Pali). It is called *The Questions of King Milinda*.

Between the second century B.C.E. and the second century C.E. Mahayana Buddhists added to their collections of texts in Sanskrit, and later in Chinese, other *sutras* which they also claim to be the words of the Buddha. It was said that these had been hidden until people were ready for their wider teachings but that what was in them was continuous with the material in the *Pali Canon*. The most famous of these *sutras* are the *Vimalakirti Sutra*, which is about a householder, Vimalakirti, who is more enlightened and wise even than the celestial *bodhisattvas*. The others are the *Prajnaparamita* ("Perfection of Wisdom Sutras"), the *Saddharmapundarika* ("Lotus Sutra"), the *Sukhavati* ("Happy Land Sutra"), the *Lankavatara*, ("Descent to Sri Lanka Sutra"), and the *Avatamsaka* ("Garland Sutra").

The Chinese name for the Mahayana *sutras* is "The Great Scripture Store". The Japanese translations of these are printed in 55 Western-style volumes, with 45 supplementary books. The Tibetans have a similar collection, translated into Tibetan, with yet more additions. It was organized by Bu-ston (1290-1364 C.E.) into the *Kanjur* ("Translation of the Buddha-Word") which has 108 volumes. There is also the *Tenjur* ("Translations of Treatises"), which is a further 225 volumes. In fact, that was not the end of authoritative scriptures for the Tibetans: it is believed that Padmasambhava hid teachings for which people were not yet ready and that these are still being found. They are called *termas* ("treasures"). The *Tibetan Book of the Dead* is one famous example of a *terma*.

It is mainly in the monasteries that the scriptures are studied and the original languages known. The respect that Buddhists have for their sacred books is shown by their place in shrine rooms just below the images of the Buddha. They have also been used as relics in *stupas*, and recitation of texts is thought to give both protection and blessing.

See also *Mahayana, Prajnaparamita, Pure Land, Theravada, Tibet, Tripitaka*.

Buddhist monks in Nepal study and chant the scriptures in the shrine room of their temple.

Shakyamuni

See *Gautama*.

Soka Gakkai

This is a Buddhist organization for lay people, founded in 1930 by a Japanese Buddhist named T. Makiguchi. Its name means "Value Creation Society". Members of Soka Gakkai follow the teachings of Nichiren, the prophetic Buddhist teacher who lived in Japan in the thirteenth century C.E. He left behind various followers, but one pupil, Nikko, claimed that he had the authority to propagate the true teachings. This group became known as Nichiren Shoshu ("The True Sect of Nichiren"). Soka Gakkai is the lay branch of this school and its full title is "Nichiren Shoshu Soka Gakkai".

Members of Soka Gakkai believe that Nichiren is the *buddha* for our suffering world aeon. They study his writings and the scripture he thought was most important, the *Lotus Sutra*. The meaning of the *Lotus Sutra* is summed up in the *mantra* "Nam Myoho Renge Kyo". Nichiren inscribed this *mantra* with his own name, and those of various deities, in calligraphy on a scroll which is kept at the head temple at Taiseki-ji near Mount Fuji. Members of Soka Gakkai are given copies of this scroll to place in a shrine in their homes. They chant the *mantra* in front of it, and it is called the Gohonzon, or object of worship. They believe that this is a simple but powerful practice which can gain happiness and enlightenment for anyone who does it.

Most members of Soka Gakkai are Japanese, but it is growing in numbers in many other parts of the world.

See also *Japan, Lotus Sutra, Mantra*.

A woman member of Soka Gakkai chanting *"Nam Myoho Renge Kyo"* in front of the Gohonzon. She has her hands in the traditional posture of reverence and is holding the type of prayer beads used by this group.

Soul

See *Anatman*.

Stupa

Stupas were originally burial mounds built over the ashes of important people in India. The text describing the death of Gautama Buddha says:

> As they treat the remains of a king of kings, so should they treat the remains of the Tathagata. At the four crossroads a cairn should be erected to the Tathagata. And whoever shall there place garlands . . . make salutation there, or become in its presence calm in heart – that shall long be to them for a profit and a joy.

(*The Book of the Great Decease*, tr. Rhys Davids in *Dialogues of the Buddha, Part 11*, Pali Text Society).

After Gautama was cremated his remains were divided into eight parts and a *stupa* built over each. *Stupas* were also built over the cremation pot and the ashes of the fire. In the third century B.C.E. Ashoka re-divided the relics and built thousands of *stupas* all over India as visual reminders of the teaching of the Buddha. In all the countries to

An early form of the *stupa* from Sanchi in India. There is a railing round the platform for circumambulation, the remains of the gateway into the sacred area, and the *stupa* is topped by an honorific parasol.

which Buddhism went relics were taken and *stupas* built. They can contain relics of any great Buddhist saint or copies of the scriptures, the Buddha's *dharma*-body.

Buddhists venerate *stupas* by circumambulating (walking round) them clockwise. Small *stupas* are made as portable reliquaries, for example the one in which the tooth relic is kept in Kandy, a copy of which is paraded on an elephant at the Great Tooth Relic Festival. The relics within them are a reminder of the Buddha *dharma* and are thought to radiate blessings.

The names and shapes given to *stupas* vary from country to country. In Sri Lanka they are called *dagobas*, a word which literally means "containing a relic". Farther east "dagoba" becomes "pagoda". In Tibet the name is "chorten". "Caitya" is also a term interchangeable with "stupa", although technically it means "a *stupa* without a relic".

The different parts of *stupas*, ranging from the base upwards, have come to symbolize progress along the path to enlightenment.

See also *Ashoka, Borobudur, Gautama.*

In China and Japan the parasols on top of *stupas* developed into the rooftops of *pagodas*. This is the Peace Pagoda in Battersea Park, London.

Suchness

Tathata can be translated as "suchness", "thatness" or "thusness". It is one of the many Buddhist terms for the true nature of all things, ultimate reality or the transcendent. No human words can adequately express what this reality is like, so Buddhists use terms that are quite abstract as a protection against anyone thinking that what is being talked about can be fully grasped or understood by the human intellect. *Tathata* indicates reality just as it is, unscreened and undivided by the symbols and definitions of thought.

Suchness neither becomes nor ceases to become;
Suchness does not stand at any point or place;
Suchness is neither past, future nor present;
Suchness does not arise from the dual or the non-dual;
Suchness is neither impure nor pure;
Suchness neither arises nor comes to an end.
(*Saptasatika Prajnaparamita*, v. 195, quoted by A. Watts in *The Way of Zen*)

See also *Emptiness, Nirvana, Tathagatha.*

Suffering

This is the usual translation of the Pali term *dukkha* (*duhkha* in Sanskrit). It is the first of the Four Noble Truths and one of the Three Marks of Existence. The meaning of *dukkha* is much wider than just physical or mental pain, sorrow or misery. It covers the imperfections of the world as we know it. The world is unsatisfactory because even the happiness of family life and the happiness given by beautiful things and pleasurable activities are impermanent, subject to change. Knowing and accepting this is the first stage in stopping the suffering. This realistic, not pessimistic, understanding of impermanence and the unsatisfactory state of the world is an important step on the road to enlightenment, the end of suffering, which is Nirvana.

He who sees dukkha sees also the arising of suffering, sees also the cessation of suffering and sees also the path leading to the cessation of suffering.
(*Samyutta Nikaya 5*, Pali Text Society).

See also *Four Noble Truths, Nirvana, Three Marks of Existence.*

Sutra

Sutra (Pali: *sutta*) originally meant "a thread". It was the term used for the threads of the Buddha's teaching, and when these were written down the

The *Diamond Sutra*, dating back to the ninth century C.E., is the oldest printed book in the world. It is housed in the British Museum.

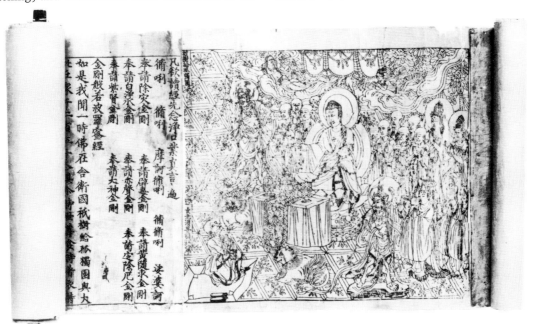

word *sutra* referred to a Buddhist scripture or collection of texts. The *Sutta Pitaka* is one of the three main sections of the *Tripitaka* or *Pali Canon*. The early Mahayana texts also claimed to be threads of the Buddha's teaching and were called *sutras*. Famous examples of these are the *Prajnaparamita Sutra* and the *Lotus Sutra*.

See also *Dharmapada, Eightfold Path, Four Noble Truths, Lotus Sutra, Metta, Prajnaparamita, Tripitaka*.

Taking Refuge

Buddhists rely for help and teaching on the Three Refuges, or Three Jewels: the *buddha*, the *dharma* and the *sangha*. They express this in a particular form of words, the repetition of which is called "taking refuge". This is used when someone wants to become a Buddhist and also at the beginning of most Buddhist activities. It is repeated three times.

I go to the Buddha for refuge.
I go to the Dharma for refuge.
I go to the Sangha for refuge.

See also *Buddha, Dharma, Sangha, Three Jewels*.

Tanka

A *tanka* is a Tibetan scroll or painting with religious scenes and symbols. *Tankas* are usually very colourful and complex and are used strictly for teaching, devotion and meditation. The Wheel of Life is a typical subject. Others are the life of Gautama Buddha, the lineages of great *lamas* (teachers) and representations of *buddhas* and *bodhisattvas*.

See also *Tibet, Wheel of Life*.

This complex tanka of the Wheel of Life shows Yama, ▷ who, like Mara, symbolizes desire and death, holding up a mirror-like reflection of life in Samsara. It shows the roots of suffering at the centre, the Chain of Causation round the outside rim and the states of rebirth.

Tathagatha

This is a title interchangeable with the word "*buddha*". It indicates that the person has "come" or "gone" along the path to enlightenment.

See also *Buddha, Suchness*.

Theravada

"Theravada" means "doctrine of the elders" and is the name of the only (surviving) school of pre-Mahayana or old Buddhism still in existence. Theravada Buddhists base their beliefs and practices on the *Pali Canon*, which they believe contains the teachings of Gautama Buddha.

The basic ideas of the Theravada are that Gautama Buddha was only a man and that it is following his example and teachings that leads to enlightenment.

You yourselves must make the effort.
The buddhas are only teachers.

Theravada Buddhist society is made up of two main groups: monks (the order of nuns has died out in traditional Theravada society) and householders. These are religiously inter-dependent. It is believed that by making offerings – in particular of food, clothes, land and money – to the monks the householders will make merit for a better rebirth. The attainment of Nirvana by a layperson is thought to be highly unlikely. It is thought that monks and nuns are much closer to Nirvana. They are freed from practical responsibilities and can study the sacred texts and spend their time in meditation. There are, in fact, different kinds of monks in Theravada society. Some are pastorally involved and function rather like priests. Others are very scholarly and involved in educational institutions. Those who are thought to be closest to the ideal at the time of the Buddha are the forest monks who are very strict in their meditation practice and in observing the *vinaya* code.

Theravada is sometimes called the "Southern

School" of Buddhism, or "Pali Buddhism". It was taken from India to Sri Lanka in the third century B.C.E. and from there went to Burma and Thailand. It is the national religion of Thailand and it is also said that to be Burmese is to be Buddhist. Communism in Laos, Campuchea and South Vietnam has considerably undermined its influence there. Like other forms of Buddhism it is now a living force in the West.

See also *Bhikkhu, Britain, Mahayana, Merit, Pali Canon, Vihara, Vinaya, Worship.*

Three Fires

The three fires which fuel the constantly burning flames of Samsara (the suffering round of rebirth) are greed, hatred and delusion. Greed can be closely linked with desire and the thirst which is mentioned in the second of the Four Noble Truths. It is represented by a cock at the centre of the Wheel of Life. Hatred is the opposite of *metta*, (loving kindness and compassion), and is represented by the snake in the Wheel of Life. Delusion, which can also be translated as "illusion" or even "ignorance", is both a hog at the centre of the Wheel and a blind man with a stick in the Chain of Causation round its rim. These three are the root evils in Buddhism.

See also *Four Noble Truths, Ignorance, Metta, Wheel of Life, Wisdom.*

Three Jewels

Triratna (Sanskrit), or *Tiratana* (Pali) can be translated as Three Jewels or Three Refuges. These are the *buddha, dharma* and *sangha*, the three precious and helpful bases of Buddhist belief and practice. It is by acknowledging their importance in the words "I go to the Buddha for refuge; I go to the Dharma for refuge; I go to the Sangha for refuge;" which are repeated three times, that a person becomes a Buddhist.

See also *Buddha, Dharma, Sangha, Taking Refuge.*

Three Marks of Existence

According to Buddhists, life in Samsara has three main characteristics or marks. The first is that it is unsatisfactory or suffering (*duhkha*). The second is that it is impermanent (*anitya*). The third is that there is no eternal self or soul (*anatman*) which survives death. Buddhists believe that understanding these characteristics gives people a realistic basis from which to work towards the happy and unchanging state of Nirvana.

See also *Anatman, Impermanence, Nirvana, Samsara, Suffering.*

Tibet

Although there may have been some contact with Buddhism before the seventh century C.E. the official history of Buddhism in Tibet began with King Sangtsen Gampo (630-642). His Chinese and Nepalese wives were Buddhist and he also sent some Tibetans to India to study. Buddhist scriptures were brought back and translated into Tibetan, and he encouraged teachers to come from both India and China.

The people of Tibet already had a folk religion called Bon. The Bon priests were hostile to Buddhism. They suggested that an outbreak of smallpox in the eighth century was the result of the growth of interest in Buddhism and the king at that time was pressurized to expel all Buddhist teachers. The next king reversed the policy and in about 765 C.E. he invited the famous Indian teacher Santarakshita to come from Nepal. Again there was fierce opposition from the Bon priests and Santarakshita left, sending Padmasambhava, another Indian Buddhist, at the king's request, in his place. Called Guru Rimpoche by the Tibetans, Padmasambhava followed the Tantric Buddhist path, which can also be called the "Mantrayana" or "Vajrayana". He travelled all over Tibet, gained power over the Bon deities and demons and integrated Bon ideas and practices into Buddhism. Padmasambhava also organized the successful completion of the first monastery in Tibet called Samye, and Santarakshita came back to help train the first Tibetan monks.

A great international debate took place at Samye

during the years 792-794 C.E. The main influences in Tibetan Buddhism came from China and India. The Ch'an (Japanese Zen) schools of Chinese Buddhism said that enlightenment could be spontaneous and sudden, whereas the Indian schools emphasized that final liberation came gradually after much study and disciplined practice of the *bodhisattva* path over countless lives. In the debate the path involving study and gradual enlightenment seems to have won and has influenced the emphasis of Tibetan Buddhism ever since.

This is a bronze image of the *bodhisattva* Avalokiteshvara, who is of central importance in Tibetan Buddhism. The many arms and helping hands suggest great kindness and compassion. The different positions of the hands and the objects they hold show the many skilful ways in which he helps all living beings.

After this, Buddhism in Tibet went through another period of persecution, decline and then restoration. In about 1042 the great Buddhist scholar/monk Atisha arrived in Tibet to teach and translate. He emphasized the cult of Avalokiteshvara and the long and strenuous path of the *bodhisattva*. The different schools of Buddhism in Tibet derive from the time of Atisha.

Some monks did not take any notice of the new disciplines introduced by Atisha. These were called the Nyingmapas ("old believers"). They think of Padmasambhava as their founder and believe that he was a transformation body of the *bodhisattva* Avalokiteshvara. They are not centralized in large monasteries or with a set hierarchy but emphasize the place of householder-teachers who live in the villages or travel about the country.

Atisha's followers were originally called the Kadampas but their ideas were taken over by the later Gelukpas. "*Gelukpa*" means "partisans of virtue", or "those who follow the path of perfect virtue".

Two of Atisha's disciples founded lineages: Marpa (1012-1097), the great translator, founded the Kargyupas ("followers of transmitted command") and Khan Kanchog Gyalpo founded the Sakyapas, based at the Sakya monastery. The Sakya *lamas* are allowed to marry and the leadership passes from father to son or uncle to nephew.

The Gelukpa school emerged with Tsong Khapa (1357-1419). Its monastic discipline is very strict with large monasteries at Gaden, Drepung and Sera. The Dalai Lamas are from this school. In some of their rituals they wear yellow hats and are sometimes called "The Yellow Hats" because of this.

The Tibetan canon of scriptures was collected by Buston (1290-1364). The *Kanjur* is the translation of the word of the Buddha and is in 108 volumes. The *Tenjur*, which is the translation of other books and commentaries, is in 225 volumes.

Tibetan Buddhism today is not confined to Tibet. The Chinese annexed Tibet in the 1950s and, after a great deal of unrest, between 80,000 and 100,000 Tibetan Buddhists left their country as refugees. Most, including the Dalai Lama, have settled in Tibetan communities in India. However, some *lamas* and lay Buddhists have come to Europe and the U.S.A. and have been invited to teach their faith at Buddhist centres. The whole culture of Tibet was permeated with religion and what people encounter is a very rich and colourful artistic, ritual and textual expression of the Buddhist path. Shrine rooms are decorated with bright symbolic reds, yellows and greens. *Lamas* wear maroon red and may be married. Images are similar in form to those in Hinduism, with many arms, and there is a great variety of manifestations of the Buddha Nature in the many *buddhas* and *bodhisattvas*. The thunderbolt (*vajra*) and bell represent compassion and wisdom skilfully set side by side. Devotees chant the great *mantra "Om Mani Padme Hum"* as they turn prayer wheels and prayer beads. The teaching is of three vehicles or levels, the first two of which can be present in any other form of Buddhism. *Hinayana* is seen as the basic moral code of not being a nuisance to the world, *mahayana* the vehicle of self-giving and compassion, and *vajrayana* the way which cuts through convention and shows forth every aspect of life in its true Buddha Nature.

See also *Avalokiteshvara, Dalai Lama, Mantra, Prayer Beads, Prayer Wheel, Scriptures, Tankas, Vajrayana.*

Trikaya

Literally meaning "three-body", this is a concept used by Mahayana Buddhists to illustrate the relationship of the many *buddhas* and *bodhisattvas* to each other and to ultimate reality. The three bodies are three different levels. The first of these is the *dharma-kaya*, the "truth-body". This is the absolute, indescribable nature shared by all the *buddhas*. It is a term interchangeable with "Buddha Nature" and "suchness".

The *dharmakaya* manifests itself in spiritual beings. This level is called the *sambhogakaya*, or "bliss-body". These beings can only be perceived by those with faith, and are illustrated in Buddhist art with the 32 major and 80 minor marks of a great being (such as long earlobes, wheels on the soles of their feet, etc.). All the celestial *buddhas*, like Amitabha, and *bodhisattvas*, like Avalokiteshvara, are manifestations at this level.

On an earthly plane the Buddha Nature is manifest in a *nirmanakaya*, or "transformation body". Gautama is an example of the *nirmanakaya*, and the Tibetans recognize certain people as *tulkus*, which is the Tibetan word for this idea. When the *nirmanakaya* is recognized it is possible to see in it the other levels at work. So the historical Gautama Buddha can be portrayed in a *sambhogakaya* form with the 32 marks. He is also acknowledged as the *dharmakaya* in a specific manifestation for our world aeon.

See also *Amida, Art, Avalokiteshvara, Buddha Nature, Suchness.*

Tripitaka

This is the title of the basic collection of scriptures used by Theravada Buddhists. It is also called the *Pali Canon*, because it was composed in the Pali language. Buddhists believe that the material was fixed in an oral form at a council at Rajagriha in the rainy season immediately after the Buddha's death. Five hundred senior members of the *sangha* listened to Ananda recite the sayings of the Buddha (*sutra*)and Upali the rules of the *sangha* (*vinaya*). They agreed on the form of these, memorized them carefully and passed them on by oral transmission for over 300 years. The collection of the further teaching was probably fixed later than the other two sections. These three sections form the three (*tri*) baskets (*pitaka*) of the *Pali Canon*. They are probably called "baskets" because when the scriptures, according to tradition, were finally written down in the first century B.C.E. they were written on palm leaves and stored in baskets. The three divisions are *Vinaya Pitaka*, the collection of the rules of discipline for monks and nuns, *Sutra Pitaka*, the collection of the dialogues or sayings of Gautama Buddha, and *Abhidharma Pitaka*, the collection of the further teachings.

See also *Abhidharma, Pali, Sutra, Theravada, Vinaya.*

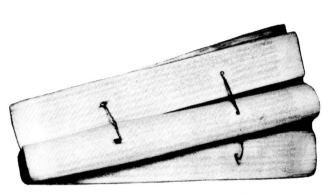

Palm leaves were dried and used for the earliest Buddhist scriptures. They were threaded together to make a continuous text and protected with decorated ends in wood or metal.

Uposatha

This is the Pali name for the day of religious observance in Buddhism. The most important days are at new and full moon, that is fortnightly, when monks and nuns recite their rule of life, the *pratimoksha*. There are also gatherings at *viharas* and Buddhist centres on the quarter days, so that a weekly pattern is established. These gatherings involve offerings, taking the Precepts, listening to *dharma* talks and meditation.

See also *Pratimoksha, Precepts, Vihara.*

Vajrayana

The vehicle of the *vajra* is named after the diamond or thunderbolt, which symbolizes indestructibility and a capacity to cut through all convention of thought and action. *Vajrayana* teaching builds on the levels of practice and ideas which it calls *hinayana* and *mahayana*. People then place themselves in the hands of a "diamond-way teacher" (*vajracharya*) who has received the teachings in a transmitted lineage and has both practised and realized them before being able to pass them on to others.

The teacher (**guru** in Sanskrit, *lama* in Tibetan)

Two important symbols used in Vajrayana ritual are the *vajra* (thunderbolt) and *ghanta* (bell). The *vajra* stands for compassion and the *ghanta* for wisdom.

The relationship between master and pupil is important right from the beginning of a young monk's training. Here the scriptures are being learnt in a monastery in Nepal.

develops a close relationship with the pupil and even becomes a kind of embodiment of the teaching. Tibetans add a fourth Jewel to the traditional three: "I go to the *lama* for refuge". The relationship between pupil and teacher is a very powerful force for growth but has to be handled carefully. *Vajrayana* is sometimes characterized as a fast sports car which can take people swiftly to their destination but is dangerous in careless hands. The pupil is taught the inner meaning of images, ideas and rituals which are, by definition, inaccessible to outsiders.

Buddhism of this kind is to be found in Tibet and Nepal, or wherever these traditions have travelled. It also pervades other parts of Far-Eastern Buddhism. Other names that are sometimes used are Tantric Buddhism and Mantrayana ("*Mantra* Vehicle").

See also *Hinayana, Mahayana, Mantra, Nepal, Three Jewels, Tibet.*

Vihara

Vihara means "abode", both in the sense of a state of mind, as in the four *brahma-viharas*, or a place. It is a general term in Theravada Buddhism for the centre where monks and nuns live. In Thailand the term *wat* is equivalent to *vihara*. In English the terms "monastery" and "temple" are used interchangeably.

The general features of all temple/monasteries are much the same. There may be more than one building or a set of rooms within one house. A shrine room contains images of *buddhas* and *bodhisattvas* and in it there is daily worship and meditation by monks, nuns and lay followers. This room may also serve as a meditation room but there may be a separate hall for meditation and large lay gatherings, for example at festivals. There is usually a *stupa*, either inside or outside the buildings, and a *bodhi* tree. The living quarters for the monks and nuns are simple rooms and are maintained by them in a daily rhythm of work and meditation. There is usually some provision for guests. Buddhists try to go to the *vihara* for *uposatha* days and festival celebrations. In countries where every village has its own *vihara* they can go every day.

See also *Bodhi Tree, Festivals, Meditation, Stupa, Uposatha, Worship.*

This traditional Thai temple has been built at the Thai *vihara* in Wimbledon. It contains a shrine room and facilities for teaching and discussion groups.

Vinaya

This refers both to the rule of life or discipline followed by monks and nuns and to the texts in which these rules are set out. The texts form one of the three sections of the *Tripitaka* and are called the *Vinaya Pitaka*. The core of the rules is the *pratimoksha*, which is recited by all monks and nuns resident in a district on the new and full moon *uposatha* days. They confess their faults before the public reading begins. If they have committed no fault they keep silent.

The total list of rules varies in the *vinaya* collections of the different Buddhist schools. The basic Theravada list is 227 for men and more for women. The rules begin with the most serious, such as sexual misconduct, stealing, killing a human being or making false claims to spiritual powers. The punishment for these is expulsion from the order. Thirteen other offences, such as falsely harassing or accusing another monk or having an unapproved dwelling place, are punished by a period of probation within the order. Many of the lesser offences are purified by the admission of guilt.

The rules say that a monk is allowed eight requisites: an almsbowl, a belt, a razor, a needle, a toothpick, and three robes either given by the laity or made of rags which he has collected. Shoes are considered a luxury in the original rule but it is accepted that the rules can be modified in different climates, since the Buddha taught that extreme asceticism is not helpful.

In addition to the personal *pratimoksha* rules the *Vinaya* also contains instructions for admission to the order of monks and nuns, for ordination ceremonies and for the rainy season retreat and the *kathina* ceremony at the end of it.

See also *Dress, Festivals, Ordination, Tripitaka, Uposatha*.

Wesak

See *Festivals*.

Wheel of Life

This is the name given to a particular type of painting which illustrates the Buddhist understanding of life in Samsara. The main part is a massive circle which is held in the grip of a fierce demon called Yama, the personification of impermanence, change and death. At the centre of the circle (A) are three animals. The cock symbolizes greed or desire, the snake, hatred and the pig, confusion or ignorance. These three are the Three Fires, or root evils, which stand in the way of enlightenment. In a strip round this central circle (B) there are often figures both rising and falling to show the possibilities for both progress and regress in people's lives. There are then five or six segments which make up most of the wheel. These are the five or six realms of being, or states of life, into which it is possible to be born. They represent types of beings rather than actual places. At the top (Ci) are those who are carefree and relaxedly follow their own pursuits. This is the realm of the *devas*, or gods. Next (Cii) come the power seekers, who are always at war. These are portrayed as *asuras*, or jealous, warring gods. Another realm (Ciii) is that of those who are passive and live by their basic instincts. This is the realm of the animals. At the bottom (Civ) are the hell realms, where beings are in constant torment in one way or another. Those who live by desire and attachment are represented by the *pretas*, or ghosts (Cv). Typical of these are the hungry ghosts whose enormous stomachs show their great greed and whose tiny throats illustrate that their hunger can never be satisfied. The sixth realm (Cvi) is that of human beings. They can understand the reality of life and have a capacity for non-attachment. This is the best state for attaining enlightenment.

Two things are important to understand in the illustration of the Wheel of Life. First of all, no state is eternal, because the wheel illustrates Samsara and not Nirvana. A *buddha* is portrayed teaching in each realm, using whatever means is appropriate to help the beings. But even the *devas* will die and be reborn. Secondly, there is no sense of progression round the Wheel as it stands. Rebirth can be from any realm and to any realm or, to put it another way, we can change from one to any other state of mind, for example from attachment to heedlessness, at any time.

The outside ring (1-12) of the Wheel illustrates the Chain of Dependent Origination, or Chain of Causation, which shows how attitudes and actions are linked together in a process of cause and effect.

See also *Causation, Gods, Nirvana, Rebirth, Samsara, Three Fires*.

The Wheel of Life.

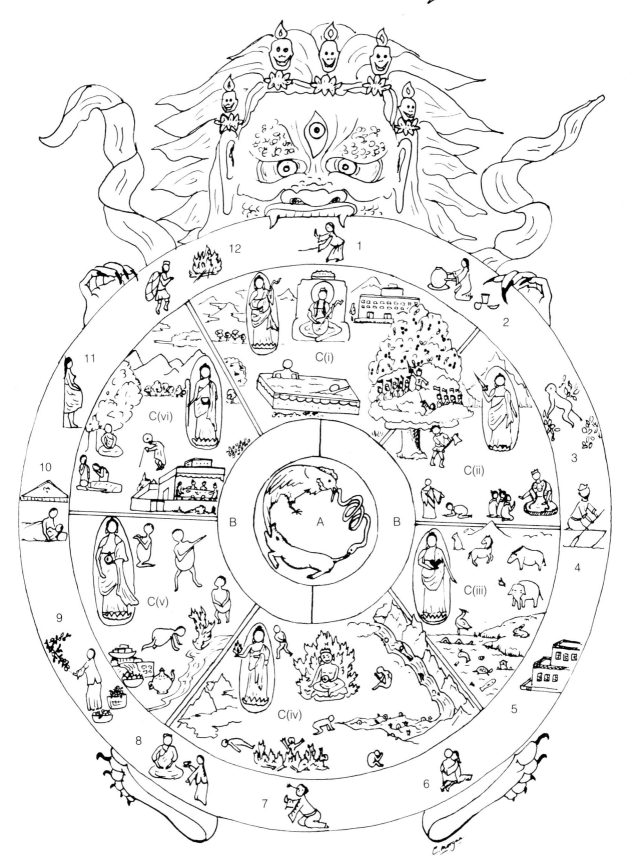

Wheel of Law

The *dharmachakra* is a common symbol of the Buddha's teaching in Buddhist art. It often has eight spokes to symbolize the Eightfold Path. The Buddha's first sermon is called "Turning the Wheel of the Law".

See also *Art, Eightfold Path, Gautama.*

These Buddha footprints and the Wheels of the Law that are carved on them represent the presence of the Buddha and his teaching.

Wisdom

"Insight", "understanding" and "wisdom" can all be used to translate the Sanskrit *prajna* and Pali *panna*. A person needs something of this quality to start on the Buddhist path, but wisdom is also the climax of the journey and can denote enlightenment itself. Wisdom is the opposite of ignorance or delusion, which is one of the Three Fires, or root evils, in Buddhism.

> The tree of wisdom has fibres of forbearance, deep roots of steadfastness, flowers of virtue, branches of awareness and enlightenment, and yields fruit of dharma, thriving it should not be uprooted.
> (Ashvagosha, *Buddha-Carita*)

In Mahayana Buddhism wisdom is personified in female form and is called "the lovely, the holy".

> She is worthy of homage . . . she is a source of light, and from everywhere in the triple world she removes darkness . . . most excellent are her works. She makes us seek the safety of the wings of enlightenment. She brings light to the blind, so that all fear and distress may be forsaken.
> (*Ashtasahasrika* v. 11, 170-1, tr. E. Conze in

Buddhist Texts through the Ages, Bruno Cassirer, 1954)

Wisdom is also called *prajnaparamita*, "the perfection of wisdom". The idea of perfection here is not just a moral or intellectual superiority but that which goes beyond all conventional truth.

> Mere listening and thinking will never make us realise the true nature of prajnaparamita.
> (*Avatamsaka Sutra*, quoted by D.T. Susuki in *Essays in Zen Buddhism*, Rider, 1953)

There is a whole group of Mahayana *sutras* called the *prajnaparamita*, and in Tibetan Buddhism the *bodhisattva* Manjushri is linked with wisdom. He holds a sword in his right hand. The sword symbolizes the capacity of wisdom to cut through the distinctions of egoism and ignorance. He often holds a *prajnaparamita* text in his other hand. Wisdom is also symbolized by the bell held in the left hand in Tibetan rituals. The right hand holds the *vajra* (diamond thunderbolt) which shows how wisdom and compassion must go together.

See also *Eightfold Path, Prajnaparamita, Three Fires.*

Women

All religions reflect the social attitudes common at the time of their emergence and growth. These often seem to contradict some of their own ideals. Throughout the history of Buddhism there have been tensions between a view of women as spiritually lower than men, whose presence is even compromising to men, and the ideal of teaching and enlightenment possible for all beings. The earliest Buddhist community (*sangha*) was made up of monks, nuns, laymen and laywomen. The Buddha taught men and women from all walks of life with an "open hand", that is without any discrimination. However, he ordained women only after a great deal of persuasion and they were put under the authority of the monks with double the number of *vinaya* rules. Added to this original inferiority, valid ordination for women in Theravada countries has now died out. Theravada women can still take ten precepts only and live as *dasa sila mata* ("Ten Precept mothers", or novices). In Mahayana countries ordination continued and there is now an interest in its re-introduction from the Mahayana into the Theravada *sangha*.

One objection to the ordination of women at the time of the Buddha was that they were necessary in the home for the stability of society. Side by side with this it should be noted that being a wife and mother in the early tradition was not likely to lead to enlightenment, so the best hope for a woman was to be reborn as a man. Laywomen were also seen as possible temptresses to monks, like the daughters of Mara before the Buddha's enlightenment.

In Mahayana Buddhism spiritual worth is less closely linked to external factors, such as whether one is a monk or layperson, man or woman. The lessened prejudice towards what is feminine can be seen in the personification of wisdom in female form and the emergence of the female *bodhisattva* of infinite compassion, Kwan-yin. In the *Vimalakirti Nirdesa Sutra* Sariputra, one of the close disciples of Gautama Buddha, says to a *devi* (goddess), "If you know so much and are so advanced, why are you a woman?" Her reply is to use her magic power to change places with him and force him to realize what little difference the externals make. The Buddha Nature is the same in all beings. What, ultimately, is a woman?

See also *Bhikkhu, Bodhisattva, Ordination, Wisdom*.

Worship

The word "worship" translates the Sanskrit word *puja* and is used in all forms of Buddhism. Worship is essentially honouring or showing respect for what is of ultimate worth or value. In Buddhism this is not a personal god but a trans-personal state, which can be described in various ways as "Emptiness", "Suchness", "the Buddha Nature" or "the state of enlightenment". Any beings like the great *buddhas* and *bodhisattvas* who manifest this Buddha Nature are honoured and their images placed in shrine rooms. These are seen as fingers pointing to reality and not the reality itself.

Worship takes place both daily in homes and monasteries and on *uposatha* days at *viharas*. Buddhists involve body, speech and mind in their worship and visitors will characteristically see physical prostrations, the making of offerings, hear chanting and teaching and participate in silent meditation.

The first act before entering a shrine room is the removal of shoes, which is a general Eastern custom of respect for a place of worship or even a home. In the West the custom is preserved for the sake of tradition and to keep the floor clean for sitting and prostration. Buddhists then place their hands together and make a prostration in front of the images either from a kneeling (Theravada) or standing (Tibetan) position. Either just before or after the prostrations offerings are made. The basic three are flowers, which act as a reminder of impermanence, light and incense. The cultural forms of these will vary; for example, light can be coconut oil or butter lamps or candles. Words such as the following are said when the offerings are made.

I make offering to the Buddha with these *flowers*
And through this merit may there be release.
Even as these flowers must fade
So my body goes towards destruction.

With this *light* which shines brightly, destroying darkness, I make offering to the truly enlightened lamp of the three worlds, who dispels the darkness of ignorance.

To him of fragrant body and face,
Fragrant with infinite virtues,

To the Buddha I make offering with fragrant *incense*.

Mahayana Buddhists make a seven-fold offering which can be symbolized by seven bowls of water or by the items themselves. They are the gifts that would be offered to an honoured guest in an Indian household. There is water for drinking, water for washing the feet, flowers, incense, light, perfumed water for a bath and food. There can also be music, represented by a conch shell, cymbals or a bell.

After these initial offerings Buddhists will repeat the Three Refuges and renew the Five or Eight Precepts. They may then join in the chanting of short *sutras* or repeat *mantras* together. There is almost always some silent meditation and sometimes some teaching given by a *bhikkhu*. A characteristic sentiment at the end of Theravada worship is the greeting "May All Beings be Happy". Mahayana Buddhists dedicate any merit that has been made to the welfare of all sentient beings.

See also *Buddha Nature, Emptiness, Meditation, Precepts, Suchness, Taking Refuge, Uposatha, Vihara.*

Lay Buddhists come to temples like this one in Thailand to offer flowers, incense and light in honour of the Buddha, to listen to the monks chanting and to meditate.

Zen

Zen is the Japanese form of the Chinese Buddhist word Ch'an. Ch'an-na transliterates the Sanskrit dhyana and the Pali jhana, which mean "meditation". Zen is the name given to a certain form of Buddhist meditation which developed into separate Buddhist schools in China and Japan and is now found all over the world.

Zen Buddhists have their own legend which links the Zen way of teaching and attaining enlightenment with Gautama Buddha. They describe how on one occasion he taught a group of people by silently holding up a flower. Everyone fell silent. Kashyapa was the only person who understood the wisdom that the Buddha was trying to communicate and he smiled. This direct and surprising style of teaching was then passed on from Kashyapa and through many other Indian Buddhist masters until one of them, Bodhidharma, went to China in the late fifth or early sixth century C.E. It is with Bodhidharma that it is possible to trace the beginnings of Zen as a distinct and separate school in Buddhism. As it developed it owed a great deal to the ideas already present in Chinese Taoism.

From the fifth century in China and the eighth century in Japan this tradition was handed down by patriarchs, or masters, who were often eccentric but always very lively characters. There is a whole Zen sutra based on the life and teaching of one of the most famous, Hui-Neng (638-713 C.E.). It is called the Platform Sutra of the Sixth Patriarch. Another Chinese patriarch, Nan Chi'uan (748-834 C.E.) summed up the flavour of Zen in the following words.

A special transmission outside the scriptures
Not depending on words and letters
Direct pointing to the human mind
Seeing into one's own nature, and attaining
  Buddahood.

The two dominant schools of Zen in China were the Lin Chi (Japanese: Rinzai) and Ts'ao Tung (Japanese: Soto). They were generally known in Japan from the eighth century and became established as full schools in the thirteenth century. Eisai (1141-1214) was the first Japanese patriarch of Rinzai Zen. He stressed the use of koans (word puzzles which often take the form of paradoxical questions), tea-drinking as an aid to meditation and the possibility of satori (sudden enlightenment). Dogen (1200-1253) established Soto Zen in Japan. Its special features are its disciplined sitting meditation (zazen), combined with certain artistic activities, garden designs, calligraphy and the elaborate tea ceremony, as vehicles of meditation. Zen provided a great inspiration for the arts in Japan, where a large number of "ways" developed. There is the way of flowers (ikebana) the way of tea (chado), the way of archery, the way of self defence (judo) the way of poetry and the way of calligraphy.

Interior conduct in Zen is not cut off from the world, as shown by its love for nature, artistic creativity, everyday activity, and social ethic – all of them expressions of an attitude fundamentally open to the world, eliciting joy and delighting people
(H. Dumoulin, Zen Enlightenment, Weatherhill, 1979)

Zen's emphasis on the ordinary as the vehicle of enlightenment is further summed up by Alan Watts in the Way of Zen (Penguin, 1962): "The perfection of Zen is to be perfectly and simply human."
See also Art and Architecture, Bodhidharma, China, Japan, Koan, Meditation, Mindfulness.

The ordinary action of making tea is here done in an atmosphere of simple harmony and with utensils and an environment that are chosen for their beauty. The care that is taken and the mindfulness with which the way of tea is followed is one of the most famous examples of Zen Buddhism's transformation of an everyday activity into meditation and enlightenment.

Important Dates in Buddhist History

B.C.E.	(Before the Common Era)
566-486 563-483 448-368	Alternative dates for life of Gautama Buddha. Shortly after Buddha's death, council of *sangha* at Rajagriha recites oral collection of teaching and monastic rules.
c.270	Ashoka succeeds to throne.
c.246	Buddhism taken to Sri Lanka by Ashoka's son Mahinda.
c.100	*Pali Canon* written down in Sri Lanka. Mahayana *sutras* are emerging through to c.200 C.E.
C.E.	(Common Era)
First century	Gautama Buddha portrayed in human form; Buddhism reaches China.
Second century	*Questions of King Milinda* text.
Fourth century	Buddhism enters Korea.
399-414	Pilgrimage of Fa-hsien from China to India.
Fifth Century	Buddhaghosa's Visuddhimagga. Bodhidharma goes to China.
Sixth century	Pure Land and Zen develop as different schools. Buddhism taken to Java. Buddhism taken to Japan and established under Prince Shotoku.
Seventh century	Buddhism officially established in Tibet under King Sangtsen Gampo.
765	Santarakshita and Padmasambhava teach in Tibet.
792-794	Great debate at Samye in Tibet about sudden and gradual enlightenment.
c.800	Pilgrimage *stupa* built at Borobudur.
868	Date of copy of *Diamond Sutra* which is oldest printed book in world.
Eleventh to thirteenth centuries	Buddhism declines and disappears from India.
1042	Atisha arrives in Tibet to teach and translate.
1132-1212	Honen develops main Pure Land Buddhist school in Japan.
1141-1214	Eisai the first patriarch of Rinzai Zen.
1171-1262	Shinran establishes True Pure Lane Buddhism as a separate sect in Japan.
1200-1253	Dogen establishes Soto Zen in Japan.
1222-1282	Nichiren.
1290-1364	Bu-ston, organizer of Tibetan canon.

Sixteenth century	Tibetan form of Buddhism taken to Mongolia.
1865-1933	Anagarika Dharmapala.
1871	Sir Edwin Arnold's poem on the Buddha's life, *The Light of Asia*.
1881	Pali Text Society founded in London.
Twentieth century	Buddhist revival in India. Buddhism begins to thrive in the West while facing severe setbacks in its traditional countries such as China, Vietnam, Campuchea and Tibet.
1924	British Buddhist society re-organized into its present form.
1930	Soka Gakkai founded in Japan.
1938	Rissho Kosei-kai founded.
1950	Chinese enter Tibet and Dalai Lama subsequently flees.

Book List

Further Reading

Ananda in Sri Lanka, C. Barker (Hamish Hamilton, 1983)

The Buddha, M. Carrithers (Oxford, 1983)

The Buddha, C. Hardy (Holt, Rinehart and Winston, 1984)

The Buddha, T. Ling

Buddhism in the Modern World, H. Dumoulin and J. Maraldo (Collier Macmillan, 1976)

Buddhism in the Twentieth Century, P. Morgan (Hulton Educational, 1985)

Buddhist Ethics, H. Saddhatissa (George Allen and Unwin, 1979)

Buddhist Festivals, J. Snelling (Wayland, 1986)

Buddhist Folklore; Jataka Tales and others from Independent Publishing Company Ltd

A Buddhist's Manual, H. Saddhatissa and R. Webb (British Mahabodhi Society, 1976)

Buddhist Stories, P. Morgan (from the author, Westminster College, Oxford)

The Buddhist Religion, R.H. Robinson and W.H. Johnson (eds.) (Wadsworth, 1982)

In Exile From the Land of Snows, J.F. Avedon (Wisdom Publications, 1985)

My Home in a Monastery in Nepal, F. Hawker and B. Campbell (Evans Brothers, 1981)

Our Buddhist Friends, J. Ascott (Denholm House Press, 1982)

Prince Siddhartha, J. Landaw and J. Brooke (Wisdom Publications, 1984)

A Short History of Buddhism, E. Conze (George Allen and Unwin, 1980)

The Way of Zen, A. Watts (Penguin, 1957)

What the Buddha Taught, W. Rahula (Gordon Fraser, 1959)

Zen – Direct Pointing to Reality, A. Bancroft (Thames and Hudson, 1979)

Charts on Scriptures, Festivals and Rites of Passage from Pictorial Charts Educational Trust Ltd

Filmstrips from Argos Communications and B.B.C.

Slides on famous Buddhist sites and sculptures from A. & B. Peerless.

Videos from Open University and B.B.C.

Reference

The Buddha's Philosophy of Man, T. Ling (Dent, 1981)

Buddhism, Art and Faith, W. Zwalf (ed.) (British Museum, 1985)

Buddhism, its Origin and Spread in Words, Maps and Pictures, E. Zurcher (Routledge and Kegan Paul, 1962)

The Buddhist Directory (Useful addresses in Britain. Available from the Buddhist Society, 58 Eccleston Square, London SW1V 1PH)

Buddhist Scriptures, E. Conze (Penguin, 1959)

A Handbook of Living Religions, J. Hinnells (ed.) (Penguin, 1985)

The Image of the Buddha, D. Snellgrove (ed.) (Serindia, 1978)

The International Buddhist Directory, Wisdom Publications

Living Faiths: Marriage and the Family, J. Prickett (ed.) (Lutterworth, 1986)

Religion and Life: A Resource Book on Ethics, P. Emmett (ed.) (O.U.P., 1987)

World of the Buddha, L. Stryk (ed.) (Doubleday Anchor, 1969)

The World of Buddhism, H. Bechert and R. Gombrich (eds.) (Thames and Hudson, 1984)

Worlds of Faith, J. Bowker (B.B.C. Publications, 1983)

The S.H.A.P. *Handbook for Teachers* and the annual mailing contain many articles, bibliographies and lists of audio-visual aids. Contact S.H.A.P. World Religions in Education, Bishop Otter College, West Sussex Institute of Higher Education, College Lane, Chichester, Sussex.

Index